D1252639

LONDON'S RIVER

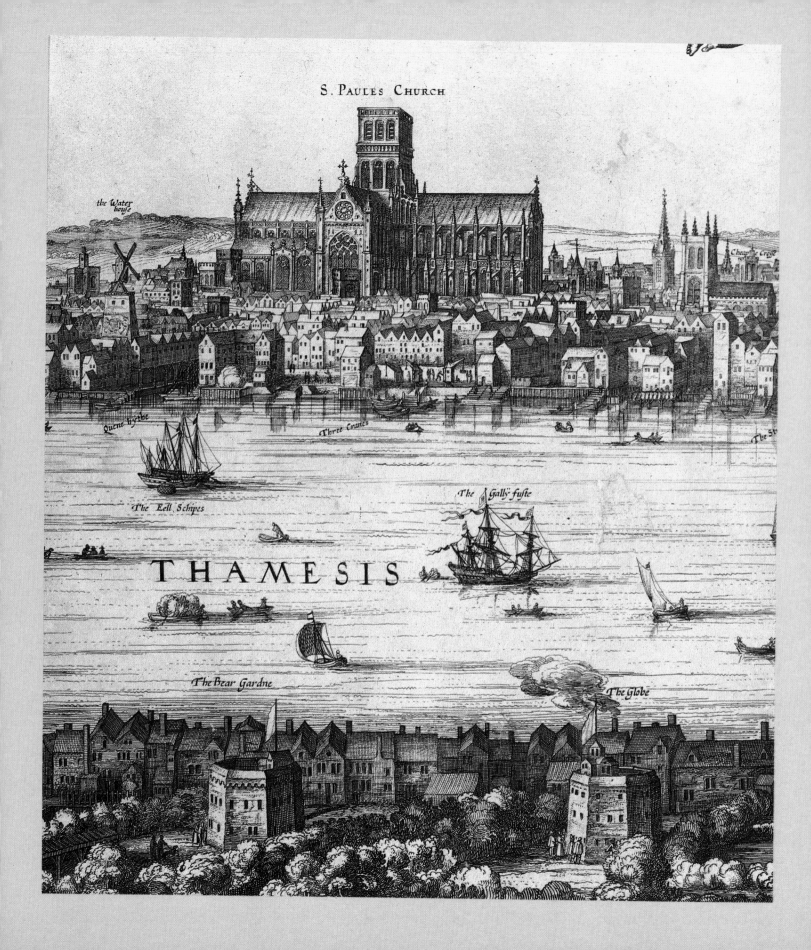

S. PAULES CHURCH

the Water house

Cheapside Crosse

Quene hythe

Three Cranes

The shott

The Eell Schpes

The Gally fuste

THAMESIS

The Bear Gardne

The Globe

LONDON'S RIVER

A HISTORY OF THE THAMES

MICHAEL LEAPMAN

Foreword by Sir Roy Strong

PAVILION

IN ASSOCIATION WITH OLYMPIA & YORK

FIRST PUBLISHED IN GREAT BRITAIN IN 1991 BY

PAVILION BOOKS LIMITED

196 SHAFTESBURY AVENUE, LONDON WC2H 8JL

DESIGNED BY ANDREW BARRON & COLLIS CLEMENTS ASSOCIATES

A CIP CATALOGUE FOR THIS BOOK IS
AVAILABLE FROM THE BRITISH LIBRARY.

ISBN 1 85145 6449

10 9 8 7 6 5 4 3 2 1

TYPESET BY SX COMPOSING LTD, RAYLEIGH, ESSEX
PRINTED AND BOUND IN ITALY BY ARNOLDO MONDADORI

CONTENTS

FOREWORD

FEW PEOPLE have a sense of history, even fewer a vision of the future. The former can, through application, be acquired, the latter is a gift bordering on the prophetic. Both things struck me as I read Michael Leapman's account of London's ancient artery, the river Thames. How quickly we seem to have forgotten its history, almost seeming to turn our backs on its waters and, during part of this century, looking on it more as an impediment to the tempo of modern city life than an enhancement, the Thames dividing rather than uniting the metropolis.

This negative approach to the Thames is of recent origin, the product above all of the revolutions in transport over the last hundred and fifty years. Firstly the railways and soon after the bus and underground systems, followed, early in our own century, by the motor car. The river ceased to be London's highway. No longer was it the route along which the raw materials for its industries from tanning to vinegar making plied their way to the factories which lined its banks. London's citizens ceased to regard the Thames as being any serious part of its transport system. With the collapse of the Docks in the 1970s, the river became a redundant part of the metropolis in terms of its day to day working. The Thames, which had been the reason for the foundation of the city in the first place because it simultaneously embodied communications and defence, could just as well from that viewpoint have been cemented over and turned into a through highway.

Compared with other great European cities Londoners have been slow to recognise that the Thames is their largest public space, a caesura in the network of densely crowded streets and jammed roadways. That tardy response is due to a number of reasons. One was certainly the polluted water that made contact with the Thames something akin to travelling down an open sewer. That continues to be rectified, although we still have a long way to go before it captures the magic of the silvery waters known to Shakespeare and Spenser upon which the white swans happily glided.

The other factor has been the absence along large tracks of its embankments, particularly on the southern side, of continuous pedestrian walks. It remains sadly still something of a struggle for the visitor to appreciate London from the river compared with the easy accessible strolls along a Parisian 'quai' or a Roman 'lugarno'. And yet we should not be despondent, indeed far from it for Michael

Leapman's book is an optimistic one in terms of the river's future.

There is a Thames renaissance, albeit an uncoordinated one. All along the riverside decayed industrial buildings are being transformed into new commercial ventures and appartments' with stunning views over its waters. From Richmond to the Isle of Dogs its embankments are undergoing a greater transformation than they have experienced since the last century. There is an excitement in the air. To sail beyond Tower Bridge is no longer a voyage into the unknown. That renaissance, however, lacks, as indeed London does as a whole, its orchestrator. Within a European context our sister cities in France or Germany, for example, seem to be orchestrated with some overall grand design embracing everything from transportation to major public buildings. Our path has so far been one of a series of separate visions, of which Canary Wharf must surely be the greatest, but with the total absence of a mechanism to mastermind the pieces into a whole. Nowhere is that truer than the Thames which seems to belong to everyone and no one. This book opens our eyes to its glory and wonder, its poetry and romance in terms of history, literature and the visual arts. It also presents a major opportunity in terms of action, for the river, more than any other aspect of London over the centuries, continues to remain the key to the creation of a unified whole once again and hence the city of the twenty-first century.

Sir Roy Strong

ON THE WATER BUS

AT LOW tide you may scarcely notice Charing Cross pier from the entrance to Embankment underground station across the road. It is a pontoon covered with white canvas drawn up into seven points, like tents at some medieval water-borne tournament; but when the tide is out these sink out of sight behind the balustrade of Bazalgette's embankment and the memorial plaque to the librettist W. S. Gilbert.

Low water makes the gangways steep, too. By 8.30 on a fine summer morning a dozen or so commuters, mostly men and most below 35, have picked their way carefully down and are sitting patiently in the catamaran *Chelsea Harbour*, also known as River Bus No. 4.

The craft faces west and, when not absorbed in *The Times*, the *Financial Times* and *The Independent*, the passengers watch train after packed train creeping across Hungerford Bridge to Charing Cross station, on the site of the old Hungerford Market, today sheathed by Terry Farrell's post-modern office and shopping complex. Many of the boat's passengers will have made their London landfall there this morning, on trains from the south-east suburbs.

Behind us, commuters from the south-west are silhouetted by the risen sun as they trot across Sir Giles Gilbert Scott's sleek Waterloo Bridge, completed in 1942. The old London and South-Western Railway never felt obliged to save its passengers that final spurt into central London by bridging the Thames, but built its terminus on the south bank.

On the dot of 8.40, on schedule, the engine's discreet thrust takes the boat away from the jetty and it performs a graceful U-turn to cross the river and tie up alongside Festival Pier in front of the Royal Festival Hall. Built in 1951 for the Festival of Britain, this was London's first public building in the post-war Modern style: would that all its successors were as elegant. Here another twenty commuters – more than doubling the passenger count – have come from the Waterloo trains to complete their journey to the City by water.

The master wastes no time. As soon as the new passengers are aboard we are heading swiftly downstream beneath the most southerly of Waterloo Bridge's three arches. On the right is Sir Denys Lasdun's grey, lumpy Royal National Theatre of 1976, a mile or so west of the sites of the seventeenth-century Southwark playhouses that were its spiritual ancestors. Beyond the National, the headquarters of London Weekend Television represents the most modern form of entertainment, and beyond that the tall chimney advertising OXO on each of its four sides is a remnant of the warehouses that used to occupy this stretch of the South Bank. Now, part of it has been transformed into Gabriel's Wharf, one of several self-consciously nautical shopping centres that were created on both banks of the river during the 1980s.

Shooting Blackfriars Bridge we come close to St Paul's, whose dome still, from this perspective at least, dominates the City skyline. Below it are two of Wren's distinctive spires, on St Bride's in Fleet Street and on St Andrew-by-the-Wardrobe in Queen Victoria Street. On the right, clinging close to the bridge, is the new black glass headquarters of the *Daily Express*. This was one of the few newspapers to stay close to Fleet Street, the traditional home of the

THE RIVER BUS PROVIDES A RELAXING AND CONVENIENT MEANS OF COMMUTING FROM CENTRAL LONDON RAIL TERMINI FOR THE INCREASING NUMBER OF PEOPLE WORKING IN DOCKLANDS.

PREVIOUS PAGES THE VIEW DOWNSTREAM FROM OUTSIDE THE TOWER.

national press, when new production techniques and high central London property values combined to provoke the great Diaspora of newspaper offices in the late 1980s. Beyond it, past the disused Bankside power station, is the historic Anchor pub, near the site of the old theatres and bear gardens, now squeezed between Southwark Bridge and the railway bridge to Cannon Street.

If the weather stays fine, by lunchtime the raised platform between the pub and the river, now unoccupied, its piles resting on the exposed mud flats, will be packed with office workers and tourists seeking cool refreshment. Not many may know it, but if they had been on the same spot 1700 years earlier they would have been looking across the river to the elaborate palace of the Roman provincial governor, the first large Thames-side residence, whose remains are below Cannon Street station.

Our boat crosses to the north bank again and stops at Swan Lane pier, just upstream of London Bridge. We are now opposite Southwark Cathedral, a part-medieval structure unjustly ignored among London's ecclesiastical monuments, perhaps because it can be seen effectively only from the river. At the

THE RIVER LINKS LONDON'S NEWEST BUSINESS CENTRE WITH THE OLD CITY.

pier two city workers get off and one man, no doubt a Cannon Street commuter, gets on.

We pass beneath London Bridge, the 1972 descendant of numerous bridges on this site going back nearly two thousand years. Just three hundred years earlier, our boat would have had to make its way carefully through a fierce current rushing between much smaller arches, beneath the backs of the houses and shops built all along it. We should have had to keep a watchful eye open, in case someone chose the moment to eject slops or garbage from the windows above. In fact old London Bridge was a few yards downstream of the present one. Wren's Monument, commemorating the Great Fire, used to stand proudly at its northern end, instead of being nearly concealed by surrounding buildings as it is today.

We cross to the south again for the pier serving London Bridge station.

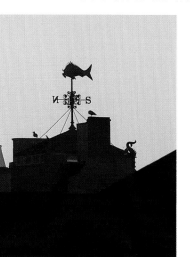

THE FISH ON THE WEATHER VANE SYMBOLISES OLD BILLINGSGATE, LONDON'S FISH MARKET UNTIL 1982, AND ONE OF THE OLDEST LANDING STAGES ON THE RIVER.

Moored at the pier today is the *Beric*, one of the old spritsailed Thames barges that no longer work the river commercially but are often to be seen making their serene way along it. Here two more men board our boat and cheerfully greet other regular passengers. On the north side is the former Billingsgate wholesale fish market: the fish are now sold in the Isle of Dogs and this lively Victorian building, with its fish-shaped weather vanes, has been converted into offices. Next to it is the stately off-white Customs House, dating from the early nineteenth century.

As we leave the pier another river bus swishes by, doing our journey in reverse, or perhaps bringing in passengers from London City Airport. We pass *HMS Belfast*, the brooding grey battle cruiser, now a museum of naval history. Today a Brazilian warship, on a goodwill visit, is moored alongside it. Ferries from here take tourists to the Tower of London, the capital's most ancient building, on the opposite shore. Beyond the *Belfast* is the vaulting waterside entrance to Hay's Galleria, the most ambitious of all the shopping and restaurant complexes that have moved into the spaces once occupied by busy warehouses.

When we have passed through the centre span of Tower Bridge we pass the modern Tower Hotel and World Trade Centre and then the former St Katherine Dock, converted into one of the first of the new shopping and eating centres, as well as an outdoor maritime museum. Now we begin to see, on both sides of the river, old warehouses converted into solid and spacious apartments, interspersed with modern residential blocks constructed in riverside vernacular, with little pointed roofs, portholes and projecting beams for non-existent pulleys. On some of the old buildings one can still see the names from their working days: Oliver's Wharf in Bermondsey and, further on, Gun Wharf, Globe Wharf, Lavender Wharf, Braithwaite and Dean. The docks and their supporting industries have had their day, and a proud day it was. Now it is the turn of those who want to enjoy the river as an environmental amenity, a stunning backdrop to their daily lives and leisure.

On the north side, Wapping Old Stairs still reach down to the river next to the Town of Ramsgate, an old pub named after the small fishing boats from Ramsgate that used to tie up by the stairs. Beyond it is the stark modern headquarters of the river police, and further along, the site of Execution Dock, where pirates and smugglers, including the notorious Captain Kidd, were hanged in the seventeenth and eighteenth centuries.

On the opposite bank, further along, is the ancient Mayflower pub, named after the boat in which the Pilgrim Fathers set sail for America from approximately this spot. Behind it is St Mary's Church, where the ship's master, Captain Jones, is buried. On the mud below, a lone treasure hunter is already at work, patiently digging in case a coin, a dagger or some other object dropped by careless Romans or their successors has somehow escaped the attention of the countless diggers who have been there before him.

A score of barges are moored just off Rotherhithe. We have passed one or two on our route, but this phalanx provides our first solid evidence that the Thames is still a working river. Further evidence now glides past us: a Port of London Authority barge packed with driftwood that it has plucked from the water before it can become a hazard to boats.

Limehouse Basin is now on our left. Beyond and to its right, the towering skyscraper that dominates the huge Canary Wharf office development comes into view. Nearing our destination, the boat turns south to follow the contour of the Isle of Dogs. Another large apartment complex is now on our right, opposite the West India pier.

HAY'S GALLERIA, DOWN RIVER FROM LONDON BRIDGE, IS ONE OF THE MOST INNOVATIVE OF THE SHOPPING AND OFFICE COMPLEXES THAT HAVE REPLACED THE OLD WAREHOUSES.

The captain asks whether any of us is taking the option of going down to the notional final stop at Greenwich, no more than half a mile further south. Nobody is. We moor alongside another boat, climb across it and on to the pontoon, faced with a stiff climb to solid ground. The commuters, grasping businesslike brief-cases, stride purposefully to their offices on the Isle of Dogs, London's newest commercial centre.

When the working day is over they will come back and the film will be played in reverse, except that by then the water will be lapping around the sea wall, covering the mud flats on either side. Nowadays the river is tidal from Teddington for the last 70 miles of its 215-mile journey to the sea from its source near Kemble, in Gloucestershire. The ever-changing riverscape is one of the many fascinations for these pioneer commuters who are helping re-establish the Thames as one of London's transport arteries, as it was for most of the capital's history.

CHAPTER ONE

A CITY AND ITS SOURCE

London, although not designated a colony, is filled with merchants and is a celebrated commercial centre.

TACITUS DESCRIBING
LONDON IN AD 61

THE ROMANS invented London, but first they invented London Bridge. Before they came, there was probably a Celtic settlement on the hill overlooking the point at which the Thames (the work *teme* simply means river in old Celtic), some fifty miles from where it met the sea, stopped being tidal. But the banks further west, at Chelsea and Brentford, were more heavily populated, because the river there was less difficult to ford. Julius Caesar's invading armies, marching up from Kent in 55 BC, probably waded and rode across at one of those two points – both have their advocates, as does Westminster – to rout the defenders on the north bank, before heading north towards the main tribal settlements, conquering them and returning to Rome by the end of the year.

Caesar's account of the campaign makes no mention of any habitation on the site of London, and the lack of any substantial pre-Roman archaeological finds in the walled part of the City confirms that it was probably then still an uncleared forest. Neither of the two most spectacular pre-Roman finds in the Thames around London is from the City itself. They are an Iron Age bronze shield, found at Battersea, and a Celtic helmet, beneath what is now Waterloo Bridge. They could have been lost by warriors attempting to cross the river by ford or boat, or perhaps offered as sacrifices in an early religion that had the Thames as its deity. Swords, daggers and scabbards, in bronze and later in iron, have been found at Battersea and points upstream, possibly made by craftsmen in those areas.

By the time Emperor Claudius's army came in AD 43, bent on a more comprehensive conquest than Caesar's, London may have been a small trading post, a cluster of huts handling commerce encouraged by the initial Roman expedition. Boats of all sizes would sail here from the North Sea carrying pottery, oil, wine and spices, and the seamen were not confident that the water was deep enough for them beyond the tidal limit.

Both Roman invasions were contested, but ineffectively. Claudius's commander Aulus Plautius, having defeated the Britons in a battle by the Medway, built a large camp at Southwark while his army waited for the emperor to join him from Rome for the crossing and the onward march to Colchester, then the Britons' principal town. While waiting at Southwark, he may have improvised a bridge across the river to Londinium and established a small fort at the bridgehead on the north bank. But since the river was then about twice its present-day width and some 14 feet shallower, the army may instead have forded it, as Caesar had. The first permanent London Bridge was almost certainly constructed in the decade following Claudius's arrival. It may initially have been made of boats and pontoons lashed together, before a more solid wooden structure on piles and thick oak abutments was erected on a site a few yards downstream of the present bridge, making its northern landfall at Fish Street Hill.

The location was dictated by the firmness of the gravel on either side and it was the southern landfall, now called Southwark, that decided the precise placing of the first bridge, for it was then the only spit of dry land in a

THIS IRON AGE BRONZE
SHIELD, FOUND IN THE
RIVER AT BATTERSEA,
COULD HAVE BEEN LOST BY
A WARRIOR TRYING TO
CROSS, OR MAY HAVE BEEN
OFFERED AS A SACRIFICE.

PREVIOUS PAGES THE ROMAN
CITY, WITH CRIPPLEGATE
FORT IN THE FOREGROUND.

treacherous, marshy, unstable area. More accurately, it was three separate sandy islands, linked by the Romans with what was in effect a causeway built up on logs. This left limited space for building, ruling out any major Roman settlement on the south side. On the north bank the two hills close to the river (now Cornhill and Ludgate Hill), bisected by the narrow river Walbrook, provided a firm base for construction, safe from flooding.

The bridge would have been rebuilt and extensively repaired on several occasions in the eleven hundred years until the first stone crossing was completed. A bronze head of the Emperor Hadrian found in the river bed just beneath it is thought to be part of a statue that once adorned it, jettisoned deliberately or accidentally. One of its more spectacular destructions is celebrated in a Norse saga. In 1014 the Norse King Olaf, coming to the aid of King Aethelred against the Vikings, tried to take the bridge but the defenders dropped stones and rocks on to his ships. Olaf therefore tore down riverside houses and used the timbers to make protective roofs for the ships. Then he tied ropes from his boats to the piles of the bridge and had his oarsmen row hard downstream, loosening the piles and causing the bridge to collapse beneath the defenders. The event is celebrated in the song *London Bridge is Fallen Down.*

London Bridge created the most easterly north-south through route into the centre of England, thus the one closest to continental Europe. Because of it the commercial significance of Londinium, as the Romans called it, increased swiftly. Many wharves were built both upstream and downstream of the

THE ROMANS BUILT THE
FIRST BRIDGE ACROSS THE
THAMES AT LONDON BY
LASHING WOODEN PONTOONS
TOGETHER.

LONDON IN THE SECOND
CENTURY AD, DOMINATED BY
THE BASILICA.

bridge, which had a swing mechanism to let larger vessels pass through. The remains of a flat-bottomed barge, dating from the second century AD, were found embedded near Blackfriars Bridge in 1962, and the timbers of a small Roman cargo ship had earlier been unearthed outside County Hall, opposite Westminster.

A speculative model of the bridge and the waterfront, as it might have appeared at the end of the first century AD, based on archaeological evidence, is on display at the Museum of London. It shows that on the north bank, downstream of the bridge, a well-engineered wharf has been built into the river, and behind it wood-framed warehouses with red tiled roofs. The city's more modest buildings would probably have been thatched.

Other details shown in the model include a tannery, a cooperage and a blacksmith's shop. Workers unload wooden cases, perhaps containing pottery, and jars of wine and oil from a large sailing ship from the Mediterranean, with its characteristic swanshead prow (On its return journey it might carry slaves, one of Britain's earliest exports, or British-made woollen garments, including *birrus britannicus*, a rain cloak renowned in the Roman Empire). Upstream of the bridge, moored to one of its piles, is a sailing barge loaded with sacks. Horse-drawn carts cross the bridge and some cattle are being driven across from the Southwark end.

Neither the first London Bridge nor the wharves could have been built without the advanced engineering methods that the Romans introduced into Britain. Sophisticated pile drivers allowed them to sink timbers much deeper into the river bed than had previously been managed, so the wharves were bigger and more secure than any the Britons had erected before. The remains of a Roman wharf discovered at Trig Lane, east of where Blackfriars Bridge now stands, shows it to have been of remarkably sturdy construction, with powerful timbers protecting the river bank from erosion and damage. When the old Billingsgate Market, east of London Bridge, was redeveloped in 1982, parts of the wooden embankment were found in sound repair.

In AD 61, in the first mention of Londinium in literature, the historian Tacitus described it as being crowded with traders. That was the year when the first Roman buildings, mainly of mud and wattle, were burned down by supporters of Boudicca's rebellion. Yet such was the town's commercial vitality that it was not long before it was built up again, with the first stone buildings now making their appearance. The river played its part here too: the ragstone used in the earliest buildings was brought up river from Kent. A consignment of it was found in the wrecked Blackfriars barge.

With the rebellion of AD 61 quashed, Londinium – already the commercial centre of the Roman province – came to replace Boudicca's stronghold Camulodunum (Colchester) as the administrative capital as well. It was a far better communications hub than the Essex town, from which there was no convenient land route to Richborough in Kent, which the Romans had chosen as the official entry port into Britain. Londinium became the focal point for most of the main long-distance roads constructed by the invaders. Another devastating fire in about AD 135 again failed to halt its rapid growth and progress.

The pattern of the Roman city is still being established by archaeological finds beneath buildings undergoing demolition and redevelopment. As recently as 1988 the foundations of a vast amphitheatre were discovered in front of the present Guildhall, fitting another important piece into the jigsaw. Nearby is the large Cripplegate fort, defending the northern border of the settlement. Both probably date from the middle of the second century, which saw the first of the many building booms in the city's history. East of these two important structures were the basilica and forum, the social centre of early Londinium, straddling the road leading north from the bridge.

The forum was the main market-place, where the goods unloaded on the riverside wharves came for sale. Beside it was the basilica, which seems to have been more than 150 yards long. This was the main administrative centre of the city and perhaps of the province, where law was dispensed and government policy debated. Its size indicates that public meetings must also have been held here. The interior, or at least part of it, was decorated with colourful fresco paintings of green foliage on a red background.

South-west of the forum, where the Walbrook flowed into the Thames and where Cannon Street station now stands, are the remains of the most imposing

A SPECULATIVE IMPRESSION OF THE FIRST THAMESIDE PALACE, BUILT FOR THE ROMAN GOVERNORS WHERE CANNON STREET STATION NOW STANDS. ELABORATE MOSAIC FLOORS HAVE BEEN FOUND.

Roman building yet located in London. It was almost certainly the residence of the provincial governor and as such the forerunner of the many lavish palaces that were built on both sides of the Thames in ensuing centuries. It has been excavated piecemeal since the mid-nineteenth century, but it now seems clear that it consisted of several large public rooms with elaborate mosaic floors and smaller residential suites with colourful wall paintings.

A riverside location was clearly strategic because it provided ready access for supplies and visitors by a means of transport superior to the road system, which even under the Romans was little more than rudimentary. But there were disadvantages, too. The river was damp, foggy and, worse, the natural sewer for the growing city. It was not long before the water began to lose its purity. Traces of wooden pipes under the Cannon Street palace, running towards the river, show that this is where its effluent was disposed of.

The remains of several public and private baths have been uncovered in the City. Their distinctive plumbing was below ground and therefore better preserved than other remains, which might give the impression that baths were more ubiquitous than was in fact the case. However, there is no doubt that bathing was an important social as well as hygienic function in Roman life. Again, being close to the river made drainage easier, and remains of baths have been found both in Upper Thames Street and Lower Thames Street, on either side of London Bridge.

In the third century the Romans built a sturdy wall around Londinium to delineate and defend the growing city, with its population of between fifty and a hundred thousand. It met the river at the sites of today's Tower Bridge in the east and Blackfriars Bridge in the west, and stretched north as far as the outer wall of the Cripplegate fort. Today remnants of it can be seen by the Tower – originally a Roman bastion – and on its northern side, near the Museum of London in the Barbican development.

The construction of a defensive wall was a symptom of growing turbulence in this distant Roman province, and at the end of the third century Marcus Carausius, commander of the Roman fleet in the Channel, engineered a coup and declared himself the ruler of Britain, seeking to sever links with Rome. When Carausius was himself overthrown by his chief minster, Allectus, the Roman commander Constantius retook Britain. He made his first landfall near Southampton, then sailed round Kent and up the Thames to take London from Allectus's northern European mercenaries.

IN THE TEMPLE OF MITHRAS, PRIESTS WORE BIRD AND ANIMAL MASKS.

In the next century, the threat to Londinium (temporarily renamed Augusta) and southern Britain came both from the Picts and Scots to the north and the Franks and Saxons on the continent. The defensive wall was fortified and extended along the river frontage, completing the City's enclosure. Theodosius, the father of a later emperor, came to secure London, this time taking the overland route from the Kentish coast.

By now the City had already begun the remorseless cycle of demolition and reconstruction that continues still: building material for the riverside wall included carved stone blocks from a monumental arch built a century or so earlier. Visible Roman remains *in situ* are scarce in London, because they have been built over. There is a mosaic in the Bank of England in Threadneedle Street and sections of pavement beneath the riverside churches of St Bride's in Fleet Street (just outside the wall) and All-Hallows-by-the-Tower in Great Byward Street. The third-century Temple of Mithras, discovered in 1952, was dug up and reconstructed in the forecourt of

Bucklersbury House in Queen Victoria Street, a few yards from its original site. Mithraism was a cult with some of the attributes of freemasonry, in which priests would don masks representing birds and animals. It was especially popular with Roman soldiers.

The British Museum and the Museum of London have good collections of Roman remnants, many dredged from the river. A silver and a bronze brooch, both decorated with dolphins, suggest a prosperous populace. Small bronze statuettes may have been connected with religious observances. Numerous iron nails, knives, needles and woodworking tools help us picture the city's workaday life, while domestic toilet items, such as tweezers, nail cleaners, needles and hairpins have also been found, as well as pieces of military equipment. Pottery finds include oil lamps and fragments of imported red Samian ware. In the Walbrook river a set of iron shackles was found, a gruesome testament to the practice of slavery.

While Roman London is celebrated, Roman Southwark, on the south side, is less well known. Yet within the constraints of its topography, hemmed in by the marshes, it was a flourishing suburb housing a garrison of troops to guard the bridgehead: perhaps the origin of its later reputation for ribaldry and masculine vices. The suffix 'wark' means a defensive structure. Two substantial Roman riverside buildings – one with elaborately decorated interior walls – stood near what is now Southwark Cathedral, and a floor from one has been built into the cathedral's south choir aisle. Evidence from inscriptions indicates that these were probably connected with the military. Having established their initial camp here in AD 43, the Romans may have turned it into their main army headquarters, their equivalent of Aldershot. In 1977 broken Roman statues of gods were found in a well beneath the cathedral, suggesting hurried concealment at a time of danger.

VIKING RAIDERS CAME IN SHIPS POWERED BY OAR AND SAIL, WITH FEARSOME PROWS.

Because of the marshy surrounds there was only one access road to the bridge from the south, following the line of today's Borough High Street along the gravel spur. On the site of Borough underground station, about half a mile south of the bridge, was the junction of Watling Street, the road from Dover, and Stane Street, from Chichester. A pavement unearthed west of Southwark Cathedral is presumed to be part of a road to Lambeth, skirting the edge of the marshes.

After the Romans pulled out of Britain in the fifth century, Southwark and London were vulnerable to attack by river-borne invaders. London's sturdy wall was of little use as a defence without the competent Roman soldiers to man it. The Saxons were less fond than the Romans of city-dwelling and if it provided no security its attractions diminished further. They moved westwards, out of the walled City, soon after the Romans left. Recently discovered archaeological evidence confirms that there was a substantial Saxon settlement between today's Whitehall and Fleet Street, centred roughly on Covent Garden market. When the Vikings began their vicious raids this town, known as Lundenwic, seems to have been abandoned and its inhabitants retreated inside the Roman walls.

The Vikings, in longboats with fearsome prows, rowed up the Thames on several occasions during the ninth and tenth centuries and set fire to the settlements on both banks. In 1016 Southwark was sacked by King Olaf's Norsemen after they had pulled down the bridge. Most Danes who were not drowned fled to Southwark, giving the Norsemen a pretext for their destructive raid. Unlike the rest of London, Southwark was vulnerable to land attack from the south. In 1066 William the Conqueror's armies burned the southern suburb, before heading west to cross the river higher up, at Wallingford, rather than risk the hazards of the wooden bridge to London.

By that time, in any event, Southwark's role in relation to London had become established. The south bank of the river was henceforth to be the poor relation of the capital on the far shore, reduced to supplying services that London was not inclined to provide for itself. Vices were catered to here - blood sports, gambling, fornication and later playgoing. Southwark often fell victim to pillage and arson from rebel groups frustrated by their inability to storm the bridge and enter the City. London's first large hospitals were south of the bridge, initially providing refuge for the poor rather than medical services: indeed, with their primitive hygiene, they were as likely to spread infection as to cure it. Noxious industries such as leather-working and vinegar manufacture were to be sited on the south bank, and in the nineteenth century the smoky power stations came here also.

THE BAYEUX TAPESTRY DEPICTS THE FUNERAL OF EDWARD THE CONFESSOR AT ST. PETER'S CHURCH (WESTMINSTER ABBEY), WHOSE CONSTRUCTION WAS HIS LIFETIME ACHIEVEMENT.

What confirmed that unequal relationship in the eleventh century was the construction of the capital's two major landmarks on the north bank of the Thames, some two miles apart. William the Conqueror converted the Roman fort at the south-east corner of the city wall into a far grander symbol of his military might, first in wood and then in stone, the core of today's Tower of London. Upstream, amid the riverside marshes where the Tyburn joined the Thames, the isle of Thorney had, at least by the seventh century AD, become a centre of the Christian church, comfortably distant from the bustle and temptations of the City. In 1065, just before his death and the consequent Norman invasion, Edward the Confessor completed there the immediate precursor of today's Westminster Abbey. William was crowned in it on Christmas Day 1066 and Westminster has continued to be the focal point of the English church, the monarchy and government. Since the Conquest, the Tower and the Abbey have marked the eastern and western poles of the nation's political and commercial powerhouse. Between them, on the north bank of the river, London has burgeoned and evolved as one of the great cities of the world.

CHAPTER TWO

PIETY AND POWER

*King Edward,
intending to make
his sepulchre at
Westminster; for
that it was near
to the famous city
of London, and
the river of
Thames, that
brought in all
kind of
merchandises
from all over the
world.*

LIFE OF EDWARD THE
CONFESSOR (11th CENTURY)

THE MEDIEVAL church and state were interdependent. Thus it was a temporal monarch – though a notably pious one – who founded Westminster Abbey, while a bishop was put in charge of building William the Conqueror's Tower of London, the capital's most blatant symbol of princely and military power. The conventional historical view is that the church and the monarchy were established at Westminster, two miles up river from London, so as to distance themselves from the commercial hurly-burly of the city, its port and its rapacious merchants; but this may be a rationalization after the event.

Although William was initially welcomed by the people of London, he was never totally confident of their loyalty. Nor could he be sure that the threat from the Danes was entirely dormant. The Normans placed great faith in fortified castles, and William acted quickly to correct the absence of any major defensive structure in London. The eastern end of the Roman wall, where it met the river, was the obvious strategic site for defence against river-borne invaders. Thus he built a temporary defensive position in timber there and, in 1077, ordered the construction of a keep built of Caen stone. Gundulf, Bishop of Rochester, was put in charge of the works. The keep, later named the White Tower, is almost square, 90 feet high with walls up to 15 feet thick and four non-matching turrets.

Thorney Island, where the Thames joined its tributary the Tyburn, became known as Westminster after the first St Peter's Church was built there - minster, from the Latin *monasterium*, being an Anglo-Saxon word for a church. It is uncertain when the first St Peter's was established. The most popular guess is the seventh century, at about the same time as the first St Paul's Cathedral was being erected on Ludgate Hill. By then there would have been a local congregation for St Peter's from the community that was established upstream from London after the Romans left two hundred years earlier. In the tenth century a small monastery was added. When Edward the Confessor planned his great Abbey in the mid-eleventh century, St Peter's offered more room for expansion than St Paul's, especially since he wanted to build his palace next door. Thus it was Edward's desire to live close to his new church, rather than any overwhelming distaste for the money-grubbers, that was the main motive for his beginning the long royal and governmental connection with Westminster – the English capital having shifted to London from Winchester under the Danish kings earlier in the century.

William the Conqueror was crowned in the Abbey just a year after its completion, as a gesture to emphasize the legitimacy of his succession. Since then, most English kings and queens have been crowned and buried here, making the Abbey the symbol of the monarchy.

Only the foundations now survive from Edward the Confessor's building, although there are more substantial remains of the adjoining monastery, housing the Abbey's museum, just south of the south transept. The core of the present complex of buildings was begun in 1245 at the instigation of Henry III and mostly completed within ten years. The Henry VII Chapel, a late Gothic gem, was built in the first decade of the sixteenth century at the most easterly point of the building, beyond the Coronation Chair.

In succeeding centuries the Abbey and its precincts were enlarged, embellished and restored. Although the essential pattern was altered remarkably little, much of the original detail has been lost over the years, to successive (and some believe excessive) restorers. The twin towers flanking the west door were designed by Wren and Hawksmoor in the early eighteenth century but completed only after their deaths.

Westminster Palace, also started by Edward the Confessor, stood between the Abbey and the river, on a site that included the northern part of today's Houses of Parliament. It was the monarch's main London residence until the sixteenth century, when Henry VIII moved to the adjacent palace at Whitehall. The main surviving part of the old palace is Westminster Hall, now incorporated into the Houses of Parliament. It still includes elements of the original hall built there in 1097 by William II. The hammer-beam roof, one of the finest in Europe, was installed in 1401, in the reign of Richard II. Its massive oak beams would have arrived at Westminster by river, probably at the quay whose remains were discovered not long ago to the south of the fourteenth-century Jewel Tower, still standing, which marked the south-west corner of the palace and its yard.

The medieval palace was not at all like the heavily-guarded private royal residences of today. Nobles and even the public had access to many of the buildings. From the thirteenth century Westminster Hall was the nation's principal law court: important offenders could, on conviction, be taken by boat to the Tower of London for imprisonment. Edward I's Model Parliament met in the hall in 1295. The Commons soon separated themselves from the Lords and met in the Chapter House of Westminster Abbey, but some thirty years after the king moved to Whitehall in 1512, the Commons went back to Westminster Palace and met in the former St Stephen's Chapel. This remained their home until most of the old palace was destroyed in a fire in 1834, to be replaced by the neo-Gothic masterpiece of Sir Gerald Barry and Augustus Pugin.

The architectural composition of the nineteenth-century Houses of Parliament, with the Clock Tower at the north end balanced by the Victoria Tower at the south, is best appreciated from the river frontage. Tour buses drive visitors across Lambeth or Westminster Bridge so that they can photograph the building from outside Lambeth Palace. By constructing a terrace running most of the length of the river front, the architects were recognizing the age-old role of the Thames as a stage for pageants and the like. Enterprising pressure groups still mount river-borne demonstrations aimed at swaying Members of Parliament: when the Musicians' Union went on strike against the BBC in 1980, a 55-piece orchestra sought MPs' attention by serenading them from a boat on the river.

ONE OF THE EARLIEST KNOWN PICTURES OF LONDON SHOWS THE DUKE OF ORLEANS, TAKEN PRISONER AT AGINCOURT IN 1415, WRITING POEMS IN THE TOWER, WHERE HE WAS HELD FOR 25 YEARS.

The Vikings, in their flamboyantly warlike boats, were possibly the first to appreciate the impressive power of the river as a setting for a spectacle designed to overawe. Since then it has constantly served that purpose from water-borne processions for mayors and monarchs to present-day firework displays staged to celebrate some significant event in the lives of Londoners.

One of the most spectacular pageants, nicely symbolizing the link between the two power centres at Westminster and the City, preceded the coronation of Queen Elizabeth I in January 1559. She had been briefly detained in the Tower on the orders of her sister, Queen Mary, nearly five years earlier. Just after Mary's death in November 1558, Elizabeth paid a poignant return visit, this time as ruler rather than prisoner. She left by water after a week and was cheered enthusiastically by the crowds on the river bank: Mary's crypto-Catholicism had become increasingly unpopular.

So successful was that river spectacle that it was repeated even more splendidly before Elizabeth's coronation in January. She was rowed from Whitehall to the Tower, where the mayor and the livery companies met her in their ceremonial barges, as musicians played and guns were fired to salute the new Queen. Three days later she left for her coronation at Westminster Abbey, this time going by road in the traditional manner. Although she travelled widely across the land in her 45-year reign, she never spent another night at the Tower, possibly because it was where her mother, Anne Boleyn, had been executed.

The Tower was seldom a favourite residence for English monarchs, except when they felt the need for maximum security. In the reigns of William I and II and Henry I there was splendid accommodation on the second floor of the White Tower if they wanted to stay there for a while. By the middle of the twelfth century a separate purpose-built palace had been constructed immediately to the south of the White Tower, and Stephen, king from 1135 to 1154, lived there for a time. Its strategic importance was confirmed when the Constable of the Tower, Geoffrey de Mandeville, switched the support of his garrison to Stephen's rival Matilda, who then briefly gained power. When de Mandeville changed sides again, Stephen regained the throne — but soon stripped the treacherous Constable of his offices.

From that time control of the Tower became important for monarchs attempting to sustain their position in the face of opposition from fractious barons and from supporters of claimants to the throne. As the most secure building in the city, it also began to be used for incarcerating prisoners, especially political ones. Henry III, who became king in 1216 at the age of nine and reigned for 56 years, was the first to make it one of his major residences. By now, though, the City of London, just outside the Tower walls, was a power centre largely independent of the monarch: the Mayor of London was one of the noblemen who had forced King John to sign Magna Carta in 1215.

During Henry's reign the Tower became a symbol of authority. His barons, led by Simon de Montfort, demanded a greater say in government, and on occasion he had to give way to them; but as long as he held on to the

WESTMINSTER HALL AND NEW PALACE YARD IN THE 18TH CENTURY, BY THOMAS SANDBY.

Tower he was demonstrably in charge. His successor Edward I made further alterations and enlargements to the fortress at the end of the thirteenth century, to bring it up to date with the latest tactical thinking about defence. Among his embellishments were a moat and a new watergate, soon dubbed Traitors' Gate, which became the most common entry route for prisoners. It was Edward, too, who moved the royal mint into the Tower complex.

In 1381 Richard II was in the Tower when Wat Tyler's poll tax rebels advanced on the capital from Kent. They camped at Blackheath before their march on London. From the Tower, the King watched the men rampaging through the streets of the capital, looting shops and homes, including the

RICHARD II PARLEYS WITH
REBELLIOUS PEASANTS ON
THE THAMES, 1381
(FROISSART).

riverside palace of John of Gaunt, the King's uncle. Next day, as Richard went out to meet the mob at Mile End, Tyler's supporters entered the Tower itself and killed some of the King's supporters, but Richard survived and Tyler's head was eventually placed on London Bridge: the traditional way with traitors. Eighteen years later Richard was confined to the Tower as a prisoner after his defeat in battle by the future Henry IV. Another king imprisoned in what had been his fortress was Henry VI, captured in 1465 in the Wars of the Roses. In 1483 Edward IV's young sons were the victims of the most famous murder in the Tower's history.

Henry VII, who came to the throne after the Battle of Bosworth in 1485, was the last monarch to use the Tower as his main London residence. Both it and Westminster Palace were altogether too austere for his son Henry VIII, who began to establish court at the luxurious new Whitehall Palace (formerly York House), at Greenwich and later at Hampton Court. But he still used the

Tower as a backdrop for the pageantry he enjoyed. When he was about to marry Anne Boleyn in 1533 he had her taken, in preparation for her coronation, from Greenwich to the Tower, surrounded by a spectacular fleet of barges, to show her off to the people of east London. Three years later Anne was back at the Tower, this time to be beheaded for adultery.

Bearing in mind the orgy of political killings he carried out at the Tower during his 38-year reign, it is scarcely surprising that Henry VIII did not fancy living there. It became a prison rather than a residence, then a store for royal supplies and weapons. In the uncertainty following his death, pressure on its cells became yet more acute as the numerous factions and their candidates for the succession fell one by one out of favour. Elizabeth, as we have seen, did not return there after her coronation, and in the Civil War of the 1640s the Tower proved of no tactical importance.

The restored Charles II, anxious to recreate the symbolism of monarchy,

THIS 1805 PAINTING BY WILLIAM DANIELL, LOOKING WEST TOWARDS THE TOWER, SHOWS THE LARGE WAREHOUSES BY THE RATCLIFFE HIGHWAY AND THE CRUSH OF SHIPS BELOW LONDON BRIDGE.

reintroduced the traditional coronation procession from the Tower to Westminster in 1661, preceded by a water-borne parade in the opposite direction; but he was the last monarch to do it. The Tower lost its direct royal connection and settled into its role as a prison, a garrison and a supply base, until in the nineteenth century it was opened to the public for visits. The last significant prisoner held there was the German Rudolf Hess during the Second World War. Today, as befits its colourful history, it is the most popular tourist attraction in Britain.

If the Tower and the Abbey between them tell much of the spiritual and

LEFT FRANK BRANGWYN'S DEPICTION OF A MEDIEVAL LORD MAYOR'S SHOW, WHICH WAS HELD ON THE THAMES FROM THE 15TH CENTURY UNTIL THE CITY CEDED CONTROL OF THE RIVER IN 1857.

FAR LEFT JOHN SERRES' VIEW OF WESTMINSTER ABBEY IN THE EARLY 19TH CENTURY.

temporal history of London, indeed of the nation, during the last thousand years, a third complex of buildings, on the opposite bank, has played a role almost as important if less appreciated. Early in the twelfth century the church and priory of St Mary Overie was built next to an existing monastery near the southern landfall of London Bridge in Southwark. (Overie may simply have meant 'over the river', but there is a seductive legend that it was originally a nunnery founded by Mary Overs, a ferryman's daughter, whose lover was killed riding to London to marry her.) In the next few years the first St Thomas's Hospital was established there and then Winchester Palace, used as a residence by the influential Bishops of Winchester until 1626. Southwark marked the northern boundary of the Winchester diocese until 1877.

Henry of Blois, the bishop who built the palace, became the Papel Legate in 1134, and thus wielded great political as well as religious influence. Nobles would cross the river, by bridge or boat, to dine with him and pay court. His was among the first of the great riverside palaces, and the later ones (including Lambeth) owed much to its example. Henry's episcopal successors continued to be men of wealth and power and the palace was regularly embellished. The spectacular rose window, which is almost all that remains today of the medieval structure, probably dates from the early fourteenth century.

As the grandest building in Southwark, Winchester Palace was an obvious target for insurrectionists. Wat Tyler's rebels burned and ransacked it as they marched on London from Blackheath in 1381. In the reconstruction the rose window was preserved and formed the centrepiece of the expanded great hall. But less than seventy years later it was again half-destroyed in Jack Cade's rebellion. Cade and his followers used Southwark as a base for their assault on the Tower and the City, as did Thomas Fauconberg in 1471, trying to march his men through London to support Henry VI in the Wars of the Roses. All the rebels ended with their heads displayed on London Bridge, but not before they had destroyed much in the vicinity of Winchester Palace.

The wealthy bishops rebuilt it every time, but ceased using it as their residence in 1626. After that it was allowed to fall into decay, and the estate was given over to housing and industry. The neighbouring church survived in its medieval form until the nineteenth century, when it was heavily restored, although there are still substantial remains of the earlier buildings. In 1905 it became the Anglican Southwark Cathedral.

The large riverside abbeys, usually with adjoining palaces for church dignitaries, were symbols of the power and wealth of the medieval clergy. Westminster and Southwark are the two that survive, but there were also important monasteries at Blackfriars, Whitefriars and Bridewell, between Westminster and the City, at Bermondsey to the east, and several more away from the river bank to the north, where development was moving as the population expanded.

But the real proof of the pervasive influence of religion lies in the scores of small neighbourhood churches for day-to-day worship. Attendance at church was virtually compulsory for the majority of the populace. William Fitz Stephen, who chronicled the city in 1183, counted 139 places of worship in and around London. If that was an accurate count it meant one for every three hundred citizens. By the beginning of the seventeenth century the City's two hundred thousand people were served by 97 churches. Not many of these were right by the river, partly because land there was much in demand for other purposes and partly because church builders have usually been attracted to hills, where their pious monuments can more easily dominate the landscape. Most of these City churches were gutted in the Great Fire of 1666, but many were rebuilt on their original sites by Wren and later by Hawksmoor, two of whose three great East End churches are close to the river.

Just how small were the neighbourhoods served by these medieval churches can be appreciated from the river today. Although the number is fewer than in the eighteenth century, between St Bride's and the Tower Wren's spires appear in profusion in every gap between the tall office

buildings at the heart of the City. Before the skyscrapers came, the churches dominated the landscape completely, as is apparent from views painted by Canaletto and other Thames artists. Yet by the late seventeenth century other parts of London, especially the West End, were superseding the City as the most fashionable residential areas. The Plague and the Fire encouraged the drift to the west and it is probable that in many of the Wren reconstructions, from the very beginning, priests found it hard to fill their stately pews. But the symbolism was what mattered. Not to rebuild after the Fire would have been to recognize the diminished status of the church following the previous century's Reformation and the intrigues that came in its wake. Succeeding generations of Londoners have had reason, on aesthetic grounds, to be thankful for this religious priority. Although their ecclesiastical use has consistently diminished, Wren's churches are a marvellous architectural resource and have found new purposes as venues for concerts and lectures.

CHARLES COCKERELL'S 19TH CENTURY "TRIBUTE TO SIR CHRISTOPHER WREN" PORTRAYS AN IMAGINARY JUMBLE OF WREN'S LONDON BUILDINGS, INCLUDING MANY RIVERSIDE LANDMARKS.

*I send, I send
here my
supremest kiss /
To thee, my
silver-footed
Tamesis. / No
more shall I
reiterate thy
strand / Whereon
so many goodly
structures stand.*

ROBERT HERRICK, 1648

MEDIEVAL NOBLEMEN built their London homes on the river bank not for the comfort or even primarily for the view, but for the convenience. Roads were poor and congested. The river afforded an accessible and often a faster means of transport to many of the places they needed to visit, as well as a supply route for the materials used in the construction of the mansions themselves. In terms of comfort, a riverside location must have had as many drawbacks as benefits: it was damp, foggy, infested with insects and, as the population grew and the river became industrialized, smelly to boot.

The first Thames-side palace was that built for the Roman governors in what is now Cannon Street. From the absence of archaeological evidence to the contrary, it seems that it took nearly a thousand years to start the second – Edward the Confessor's Palace of Westminster. Then came the Bishop of Winchester's home in Southwark and the Archbishop of Canterbury's at Lambeth. Although only the rose window survives from Winchester Palace, the Primate still lives up river at Lambeth Palace, whose Tudor gatehouse provides one of London's most familiar riverside views.

The Bishops of Rochester and Carlisle lived close to Lambeth Palace, and further east on the south bank were the homes of the Prior of Lewes and the Abbot of Battle. Not all church potentates built on the south shore, though. The Archbishop of York and the Bishops of Durham, Norwich, Bath and Wells, Ely, Salisbury and Lincoln had their palaces on the north bank. Most were taken over by non-clerical noblemen in the sixteenth century.

Great town houses in medieval times were reduced – but sometimes not much reduced – versions of the castles of the period. There would have been an impressive gatehouse on the street, with heavy, fortified gates, possibly a portcullis and a tower manned by armed watchmen. This would lead to a courtyard surrounded by domestic buildings and a great hall, a scaled-down version of Westminster Hall. The only other such hall to survive in London is the fifteenth-century Crosby Hall, moved up river from the City to Chelsea in 1908. On the river side of these mansions, contemporary views show formal gardens, necessarily truncated by their geography, with statuary, fountains and a watergate, with steps leading down to the river.

By the seventeenth century the Strand, linking Westminster with the City, was lined with some of the most splendid mansions in the nation. Just east of Westminster Palace had been York Place, home of the Archbishops of York and thus inherited by Cardinal Wolsey when he assumed that office in 1514. Henry VIII took it over in 1530 and made it the centrepiece of Whitehall Palace, a jumble of buildings covering about twenty acres that served as the monarchs' main London residence for the next 150 years. By the time of Charles II its various buildings contained some two thousand rooms, including accommodation for several of the King's mistresses. At its northern entrance was Horse Guards Parade, now stranded on the other side of Whitehall and useful only for military ceremonial.

In 1689 William III, finding the river air bad for his asthma, moved a few hundred yards inland to St James's Palace, and the monarchs never again had

PREVIOUS PAGES THE TERRACE OF SOMERSET HOUSE IN THE 18TH CENTURY.

their main London home by the river: Queen Anne lived at Kensington Palace and George III at Buckingham Palace, where his successors have remained. The departure of the royal family signalled the start of the river's decline as a favoured spot for the nobility. Gradually the mansions closed, to be replaced by commercial buildings, although Northumberland House, near the junction of the Strand and Whitehall, held out until 1874.

Most of Whitehall Palace was destroyed by fire in 1698. One part that escaped was Inigo Jones's magnificent Banqueting House of 1619, the first major example in Britain of the early classical or Palladian style, with a sense of restraint and balance that informed the best architecture of the next two hundred years. Jones had drawn up plans for an entire new palace in this style but the Banqueting House was the only part ever built. In 1649 King Charles I walked from one of its windows to the scaffold. In the eighteenth century, riverside houses for the Dukes of Portland, Richmond and Montagu occupied parts of the old palace site.

Beyond it, Northumberland House, described by Pevsner as the grandest Jacobean house in London, was built in the first decade of the seventeenth century for the Dukes of Northumberland. A square building with a turret at each corner, facing the end of St Martin's Lane, it had an elaborately impressive front entrance surmounted by a lion, a rear façade designed by Inigo Jones and some sumptuous Adam interiors added later. Even before the river was embanked, the house stood some way inland, but its long gardens stretched to the water. The house was compulsorily purchased by the local council and pulled down in 1874 so that Northumberland Avenue could be cut

H.E. TIDMARSH'S 20TH CENTURY VIEW OF LAMBETH PALACE, ONE OF THE MOST FAMILIAR THAMESIDE LANDMARKS, HOME OF THE ARCHBISHOPS OF CANTERBURY SINCE THE MIDDLE AGES.

through from Trafalgar Square to the Embankment. The lion was moved to the Northumberland family's Syon Park, near Brentford, some fifteen miles up river.

The next mansion to the east was York House, which, like York Place, was once owned by the Archbishops of York but previously belonged to the Bishops of Norwich and Lincoln. In 1626 the estate passed to George Villiers, Duke of Buckingham, who built a new house for himself there. Its watergate has survived, was restored by London County Council in 1893 and stands, many yards from the river, in Embankment Gardens, near Embankment

WHEN BUILT IN THE 1770S BY ROBERT AND JOHN ADAM, THE ADELPHI TERRACE WAS AN INNOVATIVE MIX OF HOUSES AND APARTMENTS, BUT MOST OF IT WAS DEMOLISHED FOR REDEVELOPMENT IN 1936.

underground station. Two street names celebrate the Duke's connection – Buckingham Street and Villiers Street.

The adjoining estate was Durham House, home of the Bishops of Durham until the Reformation, when it was acquired by the crown. The young Prince Edward, later Edward VI, lived here in the last years of the reign of his father, Henry VIII. In 1608 one of the first commercial developments off the Strand was erected between York and Durham Houses by the Earl of Salisbury, whose family had acquired much of the property in the area. The New Exchange was the precursor of today's shopping malls and a rival to the Royal Exchange in the City, which also combined retailing with stock trading.

Durham House was demolished in the eighteenth century and replaced in the 1770s by Robert and John Adam's revolutionary Adelphi, a riverside development of houses and apartments which some regarded as the

masterpiece of Georgian architecture in the capital. However it was not a commercial success and most of it was pulled down in 1936. Next door was first Russell House, belonging to the Earls of Bedford, then Salisbury House, sometimes called Cecil House. This was named after the Earls of Salisbury, the Cecil family, rather than the Bishops, whose earlier Salisbury House stood a quarter of a mile to the east, off Fleet Street. In the late nineteenth century Cecil House became the Cecil Hotel, for a while the largest in Europe, and the site now accommodates Shell-Mex House, the oil company's headquarters.

Next to it is the Savoy Hotel, replacing the Savoy Palace, one of the earliest of the Strand palaces, built in 1246 for Count Peter of Savoy (a region in the French Alps) on land given him by Henry III. Recent archaeological finds suggest that the site was inhabited in Saxon times, from the sixth or seventh century. In the thirteenth century it was a formidably defended palace

NORTHUMBERLAND HOUSE, A JACOBEAN MASTERPIECE, PAINTED BY SAMUEL SCOTT.

with thick, fortified walls lapped by water. When the Count died, King Henry's widow Eleanor allotted the palace to her youngest son, the Earl of Lancaster, beginning the Duchy of Lancaster's long association with this part of London. It was the home of John of Gaunt from 1361, but in 1381 it was attacked and badly damaged by Wat Tyler's band of disgruntled peasants.

In 1505 it became a hospital for the poor, and over the next ten years a large chapel was built for the inmates. This stands today as the oldest surviving building on the site. On the side of the hill which then ran straight down to the river, it would have been visible from a great distance and commanded a magnificent view of the river. The old palace was later used as lodgings and after that as a glass factory, until in 1670 it was again partly destroyed, this time in a fire, but was sufficiently restored to serve as a prison in the eighteenth century. The last traces of the medieval buildings were not finally obliterated until 1810, when they were razed to make way for the northern approach to Waterloo Bridge.

Somerset House, on the other side of the present bridge approach, dates from 1776, when Sir William Chambers designed the first purpose-built government office block here. The plan, with the gate from the Strand leading on to a stately courtyard and the elegant arches on the river frontage, echoes the original Somerset House, one of the country's first major Renaissance

LOOKING DOWNSTREAM AT THE TERRACE OF SOMERSET HOUSE IN 1840.

buildings, constructed here in 1547 for the Duke of Somerset, regent for the infant Edward VI. Elizabeth I lived in it until she became Queen, and the house was used in the seventeenth century as a residence for royalty just below the top rank, such as Queen Mothers, and for senior courtiers. Inigo Jones died there in 1652. In the years before its demolition it was divided into grace and favour residences for humbler people connected with the court, as exist today at palaces such as St James's and Hampton Court.

The eighteenth-century building was at first used partly as offices and partly as the headquarters of learned institutions. The most famous tenant was the fledgling Royal Academy. Johann Ramberg's well-known engraving of the Prince Regent being shown around it in 1787 portrays a square, skylit gallery with paintings covering the walls from floor to ceiling. That room can be seen today as part of the Courtauld Gallery, which now occupies the north-western block of the house. In the late eighteenth century another part of the building was used as the Stamp Office, where newspapers had to be taken to stamped and taxed before distribution. The Inland Revenue and the Registrar of Wills occupy much of Somerset House today.

Arundel House, to the east, has an older connection with the arts as important as that of its neighbour. Thomas Howard, the second Earl of Arundel, amassed an impressive collection of Greek and Roman sculptures and Renaissance paintings. He was patron to Wenceslaus Hollar, the Prague artist to whose engravings we owe much of our detailed knowledge of seventeenth-century London. Hollar lived at Arundel House and several of his views are taken from there. The garden, running down to the river, was one of the most splendid in London.

Before the Reformation the Bishops of Bath and Wells had their London mansion here, and a small bath house on the site, once thought to be Roman, is possibly part of that medieval building, since there is no supporting evidence of Roman occupation on this section of the river bank. (The baths can be inspected through a window by following a sign down an alley off Surrey Street.) In the sixteenth century, Arundel House was occupied briefly by Thomas Seymour, brother of the first Duke of Somerset, who lived next door. After that it passed to the Howards, Dukes of Norfolk, whose country seat was and is at Arundel in Sussex. The house was demolished in 1678, but Arundel Street and the Howard Hotel, near Temple underground station, recall the connection today, and part of the site is occupied by a Victorian office building called Arundel House, in recognition of its antecedents, which sports Tudor-style windows and chimneys.

Essex House, the most easterly of the Strand palaces, was originally Leicester House: Robert Dudley, a one-time suitor to Queen Elizabeth, lived there after she created him Earl of Leicester. On his death in 1588 it passed to his stepson Robert Devereux, the second Earl of Essex. Like several of the other palaces, it did not survive the seventeenth century but was pulled down in 1675 and replaced by Essex Street, which still has the arch at its southern end put up by Nicholas Barbon, the developer who built on the estate. Steps below it now lead to the Embankment, but earlier reached straight down to the river. Another name harking back to the Essex family is Devereux Court, with the Devereux pub.

The palaces stretched no further east because the land beyond Essex House had since the twelfth century been occupied by the London headquarters of the Knights Templar, an order devoted to the protection of pilgrims journeying to the Holy Land. It was the Knights who built the round church that still stands, modelled on the Holy Sepulchre at Jerusalem. (Five such churches remain in England.)

The Knights Templar were disbanded in the early fourteenth century and their property, still called the Temple, came to be used for lodging law students. In 1608 it was made one of the four inns of court for the training of barristers. Its sixteenth-century hall, with its magnificent roof, is one of the

finest Elizabethan survivals in London: although damaged during the Second World War, it has been well restored. It is a good example of the grand halls which would have graced many of the mansions along the Strand, just as the Temple Gardens, sloping down towards the river, give some idea of the layout of the former properties. Looking at the gardens through the railing on the Embankment, the gentle downward slope ends in a small bump, at which point the ground levels. This is where the river bank was located before Bazelgette's Embankment was built in 1862, although it is now more than a hundred feet from the river. A line can be traced west from this point, past the rear arches of Somerset House (which met the river and where two iron rings for mooring are still visible) to the former watergate of York House in Embankment Gardens.

THE TEMPLE HAS BEEN A HAUNT OF LAWYERS SINCE 1608. KING'S BENCH WALK, A TERRACE OF HOUSES SPANNING THREE CENTURIES, LEADS DOWN TO THE GARDENS AND THE EMBANKMENT.

By now we have moved east of the Strand. The Bishops of Salisbury had a large house on the site of what is today Salisbury Square, south of Fleet Street. Beyond that was one of London's shortest-lived palaces – Bridewell, which met the river close to where Blackfriars Bridge crosses it today. Originally a medieval castle, it was converted by Henry VIII into a luxurious palace around three courtyards, and for a time he entertained there lavishly. Yet living in the City was already becoming unfashionable – the stench from the nearby Fleet River was one powerful reason for this – and he grew to prefer his other palaces at Hampton Court, Nonsuch and St James's. Henry's son, Edward VI, gave Bridewell to the city as a prison and workhouse, and it was not finally demolished until the 1860s.

Henry VIII liked living by the river. He was, after all, born alongside it at Greenwich, where two of his marriages were also solemnized and two of his daughters, Mary and Elizabeth, were born. He spent much time at Greenwich, convenient for pursuing his strategic interest in his navy in the nearby dockyards and shipyards, as well as for hunting in the hilly park just south of

the palace. Elizabeth shared her father's pleasure in this, the most easterly of her palaces. She stopped there before her triumphant entry into Westminster after the defeat of the Spanish Armada, on her way from Tilbury, where she had been checking the strength of the Thames defences when the news reached her that they would not be needed.

Originally a medieval manor house, Greenwich Palace was enlarged in the fifteenth century when it was occupied first by the powerful Humphrey, Duke of Gloucester, and, on his death in 1447, by Margaret of Anjou, Henry VI's formidable and untrustworthy Queen. It was she who gave the castle the affectionate name Placentia. Henry VII later used it as a country retreat. This was not the first time that monarchs had lived on the riverside east of the City, for Edward III had a palace in Rotherhithe in the fourteenth century, although little is known of it.

LONDON FROM GREENWICH HILL BY JAN VORSTERMAN, CIRCA 1680.

The Stuarts were less fond of Greenwich Palace than the Tudors. James I gave it to his Queen, Anne of Denmark, but she found it old-fashioned and commissioned Inigo Jones to build her a house on the northern edge of the palace complex, straddling the road separating it from Greenwich Park. The medieval castle was pulled down in the 1660s, to be replaced by Wren's Naval Hospital, now the National Maritime Museum. But the Queen's House is still there, looking down to the river through the two blocks of Wren's spectacular

WREN'S GREENWICH HOSPITAL, PAINTED FROM THE RIVER IN THE 18TH CENTURY.

composition. It has been restored and furnished in seventeenth-century style and is open to visitors.

Henry VIII's most famous riverside palace is on the other side of London. Hampton Court manor had been acquired in 1514 by Cardinal Wolsey, who built a house there which rivalled in sumptuousness anything owned by the King. When he began to fall into disfavour he bestowed the palace and all its lavish decorations on the King, who received the gift gratefully – but nonetheless stripped the Cardinal of his power and possessions four years later. Henry often stayed at Hampton Court and continued embellishing Wolsey's buildings. Little more work was done until the time of William and

Mary, who were fond of the palace and had Wren design some new state apartments for them.

George II was the last monarch to spend any time at Hampton Court: his successors preferred first Kew and then Windsor for their suburban base. Part was – and still is – used as grace and favour housing for state dependents, and in 1838 the royal apartments were opened to the public. Since then Hampton Court has become one of the main tourist attractions in the London area, a pleasant excursion of some four hours by boat from Westminster.

Between central London and Hampton Court most of the banks on both sides of the river have at one time or another provided a setting for grand

HAMPTON COURT, THE MOST SPLENDID OF THE SURVIVING ROYAL RIVERSIDE PALACES, WAS STARTED IN TUDOR TIMES AND IS TODAY POPULAR WITH TOURISTS MAKING RIVER EXCURSIONS FROM LONDON.

houses. Chelsea was replete with them between the sixteenth and eighteenth centuries. Sir Thomas More lived in a mansion that later became Beaufort House, where Beaufort Street is now. Henry VIII used to visit More by barge from his riverside palaces and was so taken with the area that he had a manor house, Chelsea Manor, built slightly downstream, to add to his impressive collection of waterside residences. Two other great houses were, to the east, Ranelagh House, later the site of a pleasure garden and, to the west, Sandford House, the home for a while of Nell Gwyn, Charles II's mistress.

Most of these mansions were pulled down in the eighteenth century and replaced by houses on the more modest scale that the expanding city now dictated: modest, though, only by comparison with the extensive estates they replaced. Facing the river at Cheyne Walk (named after Lord Cheyne, a later owner of Chelsea Manor) are some of the most splendid town houses in

London. When they were built they fronted a narrow lane right at the water's edge, but a hundred years later the creation of the Embankment provided space for a busy road to be laid just beneath their windows. Nevertheless, the best of them are still among the most desirable residences in London.

The houses across the river in Battersea were never quite as grand. Almost the lone survivor is the seventeenth-century Old Battersea House, hemmed in by high-rise apartments but adding elegance to a neighbourhood that, having become tawdry, is today recovering its allure. Moving upstream and crossing

CHEYNE WALK IN THE 1870S, PAINTED BY CECIL LAWSON, LOOKS OUT OVER A STILL LARGELY RURAL BATTERSEA. A BARGE CARRYING HAY IS CLOSE TO THE WATER'S EDGE ON THE LEFT.

the river again, one comes to Hurlingham House, built in 1760 and today an exclusive club. Beyond it lies Fulham Palace, which was the home of the Bishops of London for some 1200 years until 1973. The oldest part of it still standing dates only from the fifteenth century, but Roman remains have been found on the site.

Several attempts to build a royal palace by the river at Kew met with limited success. One, the White House, was built in 1730, but only George II seemed to find it comfortable: it was demolished less than a century later. Another was deliberately destroyed by George IV before it was completed. Today's Kew Palace, once called the Dutch House because of its gables, is the only one that remains and was seldom lived in by monarchs and their direct families – except George III at the beginning of the nineteenth century, when he was afflicted with madness. He did not return after Queen Charlotte died there in 1818, and none of his successors chose to live in it. The unusual mansion, now open to the public in the summer, was built in 1631 by a merchant of Dutch descent, but there had been a house on the prime riverside site at least a hundred years earlier: some traces remain of the present mansion's immediate predecessor, called the Dairy House, which had been owned for a while by Robert Dudley, who built Leicester House in the Strand.

The grandest of all the riverside houses upstream from London is the sixteenth-century Syon House, across the river from Kew at Brentford. Syon was the country residence of the Dukes of Northumberland until their main London base was pulled down in the nineteenth century, when it became their principal ancestral home. Many of their art treasures were moved here, as well as the lion on the roof. Today it is one of the country's most visited stately homes and gardens.

Few traces remain of the once splendid royal palace at Richmond, known as Sheen Palace by the monarchs who used it in the Middle Ages. Henry VII, on rebuilding it after a fire in 1497, changed its name to commemorate his dukedom of Richmond in Yorkshire, and the name was eventually bestowed on the town that grew up around it. Contemporary pictures of the Tudor palace show it built, like Greenwich, around three courtyards, with a watergate leading on to the river. Elizabeth I died there and Charles I used it as a base for hunting, for which purpose he had Richmond Park enclosed. The palace was mostly destroyed after Charles's execution, but the arched gateway at the west corner of Richmond Green has survived, leading to Old Palace Yard, whose buildings contain some fragments of the Tudor palace.

SYON HOUSE AT BRENTFORD, STILL OWNED BY THE DUKES OF NORTHUMBERLAND.

Marble Hill House, a Palladian villa in Twickenham, was built in 1724 for Henrietta Howard (later the Countess of Suffolk), George II's mistress – which may explain why he was so fond of his sojourns in Kew. It was later the home of Mrs Fitzherbert, George IV's secret wife. Today it belongs to English Heritage and is open to the public. Nearby was Orleans House, built a few years earlier, which was, from 1800 to 1817, the home of Louis-Philippe, Duke of Orleans. Most of the house was pulled down in the 1920s, but the central octagon remains and is now an art gallery. Ham House, on the opposite bank, dates from the early seventeenth century.

Even with the truncated estates that surround them today, it is easy to see how these houses once dominated the landscape. It requires a much greater effort of imagination to envisage the parade of architectural splendour amidst well-tended gardens along the river bank from Westminster to the City, where the ravages of commerce and industry have changed the landscape beyond recognition. To that we now turn our attention.

CHAPTER FOUR

THE GROWTH OF COMMERCE

The Thames is a sure and most beautiful road for shipping. A man would say that seeth the shipping there that it is, as it were, a very wood of trees disbranched to make glades and let in light; so shaded is it with masts and sails.

WILLIAM CAMDEN, 1586

COMMERCE WAS thriving on and beside the Thames before there was any substantial habitation. The first literary reference to London is that by Tacitus, quoted at the beginning of Chapter 1. He describes it as packed, in AD 61, with merchants and trading ships – no mention of dwellings, although by then there must have been some. Since that beginning, men and women have come to live in London in order to do business, rather than business coming primarily to serve the requirements of the people. Trade came first. It is an important distinction, for it explains why the capital's commercial interests have never succumbed readily to domination by political forces.

The river and port were the mainspring of the City's commercial activity from Roman times until well into the twentieth century. The Roman wharves on sturdy piles were built out from the shore, which then ran along the line of Upper and Lower Thames Street. There, goods from overseas and from other parts of Britain were unloaded: pottery, wine, oil, glassware, bronze and silverware from Gaul, Rhineland, Italy and Spain. From other parts of Britain the main cargoes were building materials: stone from Devon, Cornwall and Kent; marble from Dorset; lead from Somerset, as well as jet from Yorkshire and pottery from Oxford and Huntingdon.

Nor did the boats leave empty. Some goods were transhipped in London: Yorkshire jet could find its final market in Rome, and Rhenish wine in western England, while British cloth was in demand in many parts of Europe. Everyday commodities such as grain, fish and, later, coal came in and out, not only to and from the sea but also upstream, where the river was navigable for some distance, although repeated legislation failed to remove entirely such impediments to shipping as fish weirs and 'flash locks' constructed by millers.

In Roman times, imported items for direct sale to the public found their way to the market inside the basilica, but there would, too, have been trading between dealers and shippers on the quayside as soon as the merchandise was landed. After the Romans left in AD 410, the old wharves were still used and more were built, both below London Bridge and above it. (When the bridge was standing its swing mechanism was much used, although between the fifth and tenth centuries the bridge was allowed periodically to collapse.) There were early wharves along the Strand, at the mouth of the Fleet and at Queenhithe - between the present Blackfriars and Southwark Bridges – so called because it was given by Henry I to his Queen, along with the valuable revenue from its tolls, early in the twelfth century.

A hundred years earlier this wharf had been known as 'Aethelred's Hyde' and was certainly used in Saxon times, when the foundations of medieval trade with Europe were established. King Edgar and his successor Aethelred, in the second half of the tenth century, invited German merchants to settle in London. They were known as the Easterlings and it was they who established trading associations, controlled the sea routes and brought some elements of organization into the use of the port and the quays. When the Danish kings succeeded the Saxons they expanded links with northern Europe, and with the Normans came further trading opportunities. But the Easterlings remained

PREVIOUS PAGES IN THE 18TH CENTURY BILLINGSGATE WAS PACKED WITH SHIPPING.

influential for more than five hundred years and in the thirteenth century linked up with the Hamburg-based Hanseatic League in a powerful trading association.

The wharves were initially built and operated by shipowners and merchants themselves, but as demand grew they were acquired by independent entrepreneurs who rented their facilities to all who could pay, and built warehouses behind them where goods were stored. The main public market from Saxon times onwards was at Cheapside, near the cathedral church of St Paul which had been established in 604. Two long, straight lanes came into being, along which goods were taken direct from the hythe up the hill to Cheapside: they can be traced today along the lines of Bread Street and Garlick Hill.

On the quayside, dealing gradually became more formalized, and areas were set aside for the sale and barter of specific commodities. Mark Lane, Mincing Lane, Pudding Lane and Tooley Street were among the best-known markets for imported produce. Billingsgate fish market, on the site of the first extensive Roman quay just below London Bridge, was the last of these markets to survive, forced out to the Isle of Dogs only in 1982.

After the first stone London Bridge was completed in 1209, a market was held between the houses and shops that lined it. Within a few years it became a notorious source of congestion and was moved south of the bridge to Borough High Street, then called Long Southwark. There it remained under the jurisdiction of the City, among whose privileges was control of all markets within a seven-mile radius. It was a market both for goods unloaded from the ships and for livestock and produce brought by road from the farms of Kent,

BY THE LATE 19TH CENTURY THE ENCLOSED DOCKS HAD TAKEN THE LARGE SHIPS AWAY FROM THE VICINITY OF BILLINGSGATE, BUT BARGES AND LIGHTERS STILL CRAMMED THE QUAY.

Surrey and Sussex. An early edict forbade farmers from bringing in cattle that might run amok among the citizens.

Siting their market on the south bank meant that the farmers did not add to the bridge's congestion by bringing their fruit, vegetables and (especially) their animals across it. In 1762 the market was moved just off the main road to an area not far from Southwark Cathedral, where it still operates today. Known as Borough Market, it is the oldest in London, selling fruit and vegetables to retailers as an alternative to New Covent Garden at Nine Elms. On the opposite bank, next to the old Billingsgate building, is the Custom House, built in the early nineteenth century to the designs of Laing and Smirke. It is the sixth on this site: the previous five, including one by Wren, were all destroyed by fire. Customs collectors operated on that section of the quay from as early as the fourteenth century. The first recorded Custom House was built in 1382, just east of the present one, and for a while the poet Geoffrey Chaucer was in charge of it.

The people who controlled and worked on the river had, from the beginning, recognized how much money could be made out of exploiting the water-borne trade. It was a simple equation of supply and demand. Access to the centrally-sited riverside quays, crucial to importers and exporters, is inevitably limited by their physical capacity, so traders had to pay for the privilege of using them, not only to the people who worked and organized the river and the wharves but also to the authorities in whose domain the goods were unloaded.

One of the earliest surviving tables of charges for using the river was drawn up in the ninth century by King Aethelred, who decreed that laden fishing boats must pay a charge of a halfpenny or a penny, depending on size, on passing through London Bridge. There was always a charge for having the bridge raised to let the bigger boats through. The commercial value of the river was quantified when Richard I, to pay for his Crusades, sold all rights in it to the City in 1197 for £20,000, a very high sum for the time, but an investment that easily paid for itself in the succeeding 660 years, until the City returned the river to the Government, in the shape of the Thames Conservancy.

The Crown, though, retained the right to levy customs duties. In 1225 Henry III ordered that all ships from outside London should unload their fish, grain and other commodities upstream of the bridge at Queenhithe, and that a duty should be paid. This edict, however, seems to have proved largely ineffective, and the fishing boats continued to unload at Billingsgate before they reached the bridge. Fifty years later Edward I imposed duties of half a mark on a sack of wool and one mark on a last of leather. Wool, then England's most important product, would come into London down the coast from East Anglia or down the river from the Midlands, and much of it, after the duty had been paid, would be sent for export to the Staple in Calais, northern Europe's principal commodity market.

John Stow, in his *Survey of London* (1598), records that:

GEOFFREY CHAUCER, 14TH CENTURY POET AND, BRIEFLY, CHIEF CUSTOMS OFFICER.

RIGHT SAMUEL SCOTT'S PICTURE OF CUSTOM HOUSE QUAY IN THE MID-18TH CENTURY SHOWS THE REVENUE OFFICER NEGOTIATING WITH TRADERS FOR IMPORT DUTIES.

Touching the ancient customs of Billingsgate, in the reign of Edward III, every great ship landing there paid for standage twopence, every little ship with oarlocks a penny, the lesser boat called a battle a halfpenny; of two quarters of corn measured the king was to have one farthing, of a combe of corn a penny, of every weight going out of the city a halfpenny, of two quarters of sea coal measured a farthing and of every tun of ale going out of England beyond the seas, by merchant strangers, fourpence, of every thousand herrings a farthing.

Sea coal had begun to be shipped into London from north-east England by the thirteenth century and possibly earlier, and for centuries it was the commonest commodity seen on the Thames. It was called sea coal to distinguish it from charcoal. The usual explanation of the name is that it was coal that arrived by sea, but an alternative theory has it that the earliest supplies were retrieved from the coast. Old Seacoal Lane, off Farringdon Street, once led to an inlet off the Fleet River where the coal barges were unloaded. At the beginning of the seventeenth century two hundred colliers

operated in the Thames; by 1850 the figure was up to at least twelve hundred, many of them directly serving the new industries that had grown alongside the river. (Henry Mayhew, writing in 1861, quotes a figure more than twice as high.) The Coal Exchange, a splendid Victorian building next to the Custom House, was demolished in 1962.

The volume of river traffic from the earliest times meant that most ships could not be accommodated at the quays but had to anchor in midstream and pay lightermen to take their cargoes ashore. The lightermen manoeuvred the heavy barges that carried the goods, exploiting the tides for their main motive power and using 25-foot oars for steering. They were distinct from the watermen, who ferried passengers in light wherries.

The shipowners then had to pay the porters to unload them. The more they paid, the faster they could get their cargoes ashore and new goods loaded – in other words the more business they could do. As traffic increased, the trade became even harder to control. The lack of competent regulation led to smuggling, theft and a great deal of corruption. Like rail travellers arriving at a crowded and confusing terminus, the skippers of merchant ships would be met by people who would claim to be able to help them, in this case by getting them and their cargoes quickly on to shore. Sometimes they could achieve this by using unofficial landing places below the Tower of London, not properly policed by the city. Occasionally the 'agents' were simply swindlers.

The first attempt to control these abuses came in Elizabethan times with the establishment of twenty 'legal quays' on the 500-yard stretch of shoreline between the Bridge and the Tower, where customs duties were levied. Each of the quays was named after the person who operated it – Chester's Quay, Smart's Quay, etc. It was forbidden to land goods anywhere else, or to unload anything anywhere in the hours of darkness, except fish.

LICENSED WATERMEN WORE A DISTINCTIVE BADGE ON THEIR ARM FOR IDENTIFICATION.

When this produced ever greater congestion and delays, without noticeably reducing the corruption, extra 'sufferance wharves' were opened after 1663, some below the Tower. The removal of the two middle arches of London Bridge in 1759 meant that larger ships than before could carry their cargoes to the wharves beyond the bridge, but they still had to clear customs at the authorized points. Shippers continued to complain of delays, pilfering and overcharging by wharf-owners. Customs officers were sometimes in league with the thieves, delaying the clearance of goods to allow time for them to be spirited away.

The people who benefited most from the explosion of activity were those engaged directly in river trades such as pilots, watermen, lightermen and porters. With growing congestion on the river, the provision of properly trained pilots, to steer ships through the hazards of the Thames Estuary, was clearly all-important. The job required not only a detailed knowledge of the

topography of the river but also of the tides, for in the days of sail, with winds being unpredictable in direction and force, the boats relied largely on the tidal flow to get them up and down river.

In 1514 Henry VIII granted a charter to Trinity House to train and appoint pilots all over England and to place buoys and lights in estuaries and along coasts. Trinity House was a seafarers' institute, named after the parish in Deptford where it was initially based, close to Henry's great naval dockyard. In 1593 it was granted an additional monopoly of providing ballast to ships leaving London empty: sand and gravel were dredged from the river bed for the purpose, thus keeping the channel clear at the same time. Trinity House gave up its ballastage rights in 1694 but is still the authority responsible for pilots, lighthouses and marine safety.

The porters were first organized in the thirteenth century, from when there are records of a brotherhood of corn and salt porters at Queenhithe. Later, separate groups were formed to handle specific aspects of the work on the quays – for instance, different porters worked on British and foreign ships, and some were authorized to weigh goods as well as carry them. There were also street porters, who bore the unloaded goods from the wharves to the City markets. Demarcation disputes arose constantly. Some of the old labour practices were maintained when the docks were built and the work force unionized in the nineteenth century.

The watermen formed their guild in 1555 and admitted lightermen a century-and-a-half later. They had to serve a seven-year apprenticeship before being granted the large metal badge to wear on their arms, to show that they were qualified. Watermen had a reputation for being arrogant, garrulous, uncouth and abusive, with the habit of whistling nonchalantly to show contempt for their customers and, especially, for their rival boatmen, towards whom it was the custom to shout insults as they passed. When they were for hire they would congregate by one of the innumerable flights of river stairs and press their services on potential passengers, who would point to the man selected – there was nothing so orderly as a first-come-first hired taxi rank. According to a contemporary account, the men not chosen would then turn on the lucky one who was, shouting abuse.

Yet for the most part the hostility was feigned, for men working on the river or at sea rely more than most other tradesmen on each other's generosity. In an environment stiff with natural and possibly fatal hazards, co-operation and mutual understanding are essential tools of survival. This is why boatmen have always placed great emphasis on camaraderie and collective support and have jealously protected entry into their ranks. It was, too, an insecure way of life, for they were always vulnerable to press gangs seeking to recruit experienced hands for the latest royal naval adventure. The

ABOVE THE 18TH CENTURY CUSTOM HOUSE, DESTROYED BY FIRE IN 1814.

FAR LEFT IN 1820 THE WATERMEN PRESENTED AN ADDRESS OF LOYALTY TO QUEEN CAROLINE, SPURNED WIFE OF THE NEW KING GEORGE IV, AT BRANDENBURGH HOUSE, HAMMERSMITH.

watermen's tradition survives today in the contest for Doggett's Coat and Badge, an annual rowing race for novice watermen from London Bridge to Chelsea instituted by Tom Doggett, an actor, in 1716, as a mark of gratitude to a waterman who had rowed him home to Chelsea on a rough night, against the tide. (Lightermen working the Thames still have to join the Watermen's Company.)

Apart from trips along and across the river, from one flight of stairs to another, watermen offered a variety of specialized river services, of which the most spectacular was bridge shooting, undertaken by men skilled in navigating the fast-flowing waters beneath London Bridge. Because the stanchions of the bridge were close together, and the channels between them narrow, the water would rush through as if over a weir, like the rapids below a waterfall. The effect was heightened when, at the end of the sixteenth century, water-mills were placed beneath many of the bridge's arches to supply water to the City. Many boatmen and passengers lost their lives in the attempt to shoot the rapids, but an expert waterman would – at a price – take a boat through while passengers, for safety, left the craft before it reached the bridge and proceeded on foot until it had been safely taken through the dangerous waters.

Despite the growing congestion on the Thames, the watermen constituted a powerful lobby against roads and additional bridges and complained vociferously when travel by coach overland began to supersede travel by water. Stow says that the first coach was introduced to England in 1564 by a Dutchman, William Boonen, coachman to Queen Elizabeth,

> and after a while divers great ladies, with as great jealousy of the Queen's displeasure, made them coaches, and rid in them up and down the country, to the great admiration of all the beholders; but then by little and little they grew usual among the nobility, and others of sort, and within twenty years became a great trade of coach making.

In 1614 the watermen sponsored a bill in Parliament to have 'outrageous coaches' banned by law, but although it was rejected the campaign was sustained, partly through the efforts of their eloquent spokesman John Taylor, the watermen's poet. His views on 'upstart hellcart-coaches' were pungently expressed in this verse, published in 1630:

> Carroaches, coaches, jades and Flanders mares
> Doe rob us of our shares, our wares, our fares;
> Against the ground we stand and knocke our heeles,
> Whilest all our profit runs away on wheels:
> And whosoever but observes and notes
> The great increase of coaches and of boates,
> Shall find their number more than e'er they were
> By half and more within these thirty yeeres.

ROWLANDSON'S PORTRAYAL
OF THE HAZARDS OF
ENGAGING A WATERMAN, AS
HORDES OF THEM GATHER
AT THE RIVER STAIRS,
LOUDLY CALLING FOR
CUSTOM AND ABUSING THEIR
RIVALS.

Apart from the constantly improving road services, the main reason for this sudden development of alternative means of transport was London's rapidly expanding population. In the forty years between 1560 and 1600 the number of inhabitants more than doubled to some 200,000. The city authorities were alarmed by this but could do nothing to stop people from all over the country coming to seek their fortune in the city.

Those with skills set themselves up in business, often near the waterfront, now teeming with merchants and other prospective customers. For those whose crafts were directly connected with maritime trade, such as coopers and sailmakers, there was no other sensible place to do business, but even blacksmiths and tailors, for example, found profit in establishing themselves in this, the commercial heart of the capital. The great majority of the newcomers, however, had no such skills. They had to make a living as best they could, resorting, at the lowest end of the scale, to crime and beggary. These occupations, too, are best practised where most people congregate, so they further swelled the crowds on the quaysides and found accommodation in the slums that quickly grew around the east of the Tower.

Some of the easiest money was to be had catering to the singular needs of the growing number of sailors who manned the vessels using the harbour. The streets near the quays were crammed with cheap lodgings for sailors: Mincing Lane specialized in accommodating foreign seamen in rooms above its shops and busy market. Stow reports that by the end of the sixteenth century Ratcliff Highway, between the Tower and Limehouse, was lined with taverns, brothels, doss-houses and the other goods and services demanded through the ages by men coming ashore after lengthy spells at sea. It became known as 'sailortown' and was decidedly not a place where respectable citizens would want to be seen.

The great increase in land traffic caused by the population growth put extra pressure on London Bridge. There was a clear need for at least one alternative crossing; but the powerful watermen succeeded in delaying any such development until the middle of the eighteenth century. They were tenacious in their attempts to sustain their monopoly by employing what today would be seen as blatant restrictive practices.

In 1613 the City of London still maintained a ban on theatres within its limits and the watermen did a lively trade in ferrying playgoers across the river to see Shakespeare's, Jonson's and Marlowe's latest successes. When actors petitioned to be allowed to open a theatre north of the river the watermen protested vigorously, saying it would harm their income and reduce their numbers, which would be against the national interest, given that they were such an important source of recruitment for the Royal Navy. The players responded satirically by proposing that the Royal Exchange and other important institutions be shifted south of the river for the benefit of the watermen. Nonetheless, on this occasion the watermen won the day.

The Royal Exchange was one of the institutions created to satisfy the increasingly sophisticated requirements of the business spawned by the river. In 1568 Sir Thomas Gresham, a mercer, established it, on the hill above London Bridge, as a clearing house for trading of all kinds. Businessmen would negotiate for cargoes and arrange financing for further voyages. Before the exchange was built the traders used to congregate to do business in Lombard Street, so called because many of the merchants were from Lombardy. The new exchange served many other commercial purposes. It became the place to settle debts when they became due – something that had formerly been done at the font of old St Paul's Cathedral. There were, too, retail shops. The Royal Exchange fulfilled many of the functions of the basilica that had stood a few hundred yards away in Roman times.

SYMBOLS OF COMMERCIAL POWER: THE BANK OF ENGLAND AND ROYAL EXCHANGE, 1861.

Shipping itself now became big business. In the seventeenth century the ships' owners and masters would meet exporters in designated coffee-houses to match their cargo requirements with capacity, routes and dates. This soon became formalized as the Baltic Exchange, which today is the international centre for the leasing of ships and cargo space, and also deals with air freight. As trade expanded and ships penetrated to ever more distant and perilous parts of the globe, their owners wanted to insure their vessels and cargoes against loss. So great were the risks that the merchants formed syndicates to underwrite the insurance. They met to transact this business at Edward Lloyd's coffee-house in the City, later at the New Lloyds coffee-house and briefly at the Royal Exchange. News of shipping was published in a newspaper called *Lloyd's List*. When a formal institution was created for insuring ships it borrowed Lloyd's name and is now the world's main clearing house for insurance of all kinds, operating from one of the most admired modern office buildings in the City.

LLOYD'S COFFEE HOUSE, WHERE MERCHANTS GATHERED TO TRANSACT MARINE INSURANCE BEFORE A FORMAL ORGANISATION – NAMED AFTER LLOYD'S – WAS ESTABLISHED FOR THE PURPOSE.

Money for the transaction of business was coined at the mint in the Tower and distributed at Old Change, or the Old Exchange, just south of St Paul's. It soon became clear that some kind of banking system was a necessary adjunct to trade. At first it was supplied by the goldsmiths, until dedicated banks were established in the seventeenth century: Child's at Temple Bar, Hoare's in Fleet Street and Snow's in the Strand. In 1694 the Bank of England was created, primarily to finance the war against France. It first set up shop in Mercers' Hall in Cheapside, then Grocers' Hall in Poultry, before occupying its present site in Threadneedle Street in 1734. Symbolizing the dependence of finance on river-borne commerce, the Bank installed a wind dial in its grand courtroom in 1805, so one could tell how quickly the merchantmen from the East and West Indies would be able to sail up the Thames and begin unloading their lucrative cargoes. The dial is still there, if today seldom consulted.

To do business profitably, merchants required not just good winds and a reliable source of finance but also swift and accurate intelligence from home and overseas. The newspaper industry was established in London in the eighteenth century primarily to supply that need. The *Daily Courant*, which began in 1702, is widely accepted as the first British daily paper. It was, at the beginning, made up of stories extracted from European newspapers which might have an impact on foreign trade. It had its headquarters near Ludgate Hill, a few yards from the river and from London's growing commercial centre, setting a precedent for the siting of newspapers in the Fleet Street area, close both to their main customers and the source of their foreign news – the overseas journals arriving in London by boat. (The printing trade was already well established on both sides of the river: London's first printer, Wynkyn de

Worde, had set up his press near St Bride's Church in 1500.) *The Times*, founded in 1785 as the *Daily Universal Register*, was the most powerful daily paper for a century, and owed its pre-eminence to its overseas news service. All papers devoted much space to listing the arrival and departure of ships at London and other ports: *Lloyd's List*, of course, carried little else.

With the beginnings of the Industrial Revolution and the British Empire, there was a growing amount of trade to be done but precious little space in which to do it. The clear danger was that London would lose its status as the major southern port to its burgeoning rivals, Bristol and Plymouth. After a fierce political battle, and against the firm opposition of the vested interests, legislation for the construction of the first of the enclosed dockyards, the West India Dock, was passed in 1799. As the nineteenth century began, the geography and economy of east London were about to be transformed.

THE UNDERWRITING ROOM AT LLOYD'S IN 1948, PAINTED BY TERENCE CUNEO.

An array of tall chimneys – each one a guide-post to some large manufacturing establishment beneath – here a brewery, there a sawmill, farther on a hat factory, a distillery, a vinegar factory and numerous others. Southwark is as distinguishable for its tall chimneys and clouds of smoke emitted by them, as London for its church spires.

GEORGE DODD, 1843

UNTIL THE advent of the railways, a riverside location was essential for the manufacture of any items of substantial size, or made from bulky raw materials. The river was far and away the most efficient route for bringing in supplies and taking out finished goods, as well as providing power to work the machinery and a convenient – if often unhygienic – repository for effluent and waste. Building boats and ships has been a riverside occupation since navigation began, and boatbuilders of various sizes sprang up along the Thames. The construction of larger seagoing vessels was naturally confined to the lower reaches, below London Bridge, where the river was broader and its bends created suitable sites for docks and harbours. Rotherhithe, Deptford, Greenwich, Woolwich and Erith, all on the south bank, boasted substantial shipyards from Tudor times and earlier.

Henry VIII is generally credited with having started the construction and repair of large ships on the Thames, but in 1475 Edward IV had already launched a battle fleet there to carry troops to invade France. It was Henry, though, who decided that the nation's prosperity and influence depended on sea power, and the largest ships ever seen in England were built for his navy. His giant flagship *Henri Grâce à Dieu*, known in awe as the Great Harry, was laid down at Erith, where Italian shipbuilders had to be imported because the locals had never worked on anything as big. The ship, launched with spectacular ceremony at Greenwich in 1514, was fitted out at Deptford, where Henry was creating the country's largest shipyard for building and equipping his navy. Next to it was a victualling yard, where ships took on supplies: the diarist Samuel Pepys had responsibility for it from 1665 to 1679.

Henry established a second shipyard at Woolwich in 1515, and most of Britain's warships were built along this stretch of the Thames until 1869, when the yards were closed. By this time modern shipbuilding required deeper docks, and the use of iron instead of timber made it more sensible to build in the north of Britain. The Thames Ironworks and Shipbuilding Company on Bow Creek had the distinction of building the first ironclad warship, *HMS Warrior*, in 1860; but it closed in 1912 after completing the last Royal Navy vessel to be launched on the river, *HMS Thunderer*.

Shipbuilding for the navy was not the only warlike industry on the Thames. Armour was still essential for military operations on land, and Henry established factories for it first at Southwark and later at Greenwich and Lewisham, again manned by experienced European craftsmen. Cannon had been made at the Tower of London since the fourteenth century, and lead shot was manufactured at various London sites. (The shot tower that stood on the Festival of Britain site near Waterloo Station was built much later, in 1826.)

Gunpowder was made at the Rotherhithe water-mills from Tudor times. A Rotherhithe man, Francis Lee, was appointed gunpowder maker to Elizabeth I. The powder was later made at Greenwich and Woolwich, which became the main storage place for major military equipment and, in 1717, the centre for its manufacture also. Woolwich Arsenal, called the Royal Arsenal from 1805, expanded to become London's largest manufacturing complex by the time of the First World War, employing 75,000 people on 1200 acres. Today more than half of that area is still the property of the Ministry of Defence, and access to its fine early eighteenth-century buildings is restricted.

As trade expanded, big ships were required for civilian as well as military use, and larger commercial shipyards were established on both sides of the river below the Tower. In 1612 the immense Blackwall yard was opened just east of the Isle of Dogs, and dominated London shipbuilding, making both warships and cargo vessels, until it closed in 1907. The Victorian writer George Dodd visited this yard when writing his 1843 book, *Days at the Factories*. He traced its ownership to Cromwellian times, when it belonged to Sir Henry Johnson, 'a liberal man who seems to have contributed much to the improvement and benefit of the neighbouring hamlet of Poplar'.

At least fifteen men-o'-war, each carrying fifty to seventy guns, were built there in the second half of the seventeenth century, and during the next hundred years more warships were constructed for engagements in America and elsewhere. In 1839 some early experiments with steam power were made here, and in the 1860s the yard began making iron ships as well as wooden frigates and clippers. Its main commercial customer was the East India Company, many of whose largest vessels were built here.

A feature of the yard, and a prominent landmark along the Thames until it

THE LAUNCH IN 1831 OF *HMS THUNDERER*, ONE OF MANY WOOLWICH-BUILT WARSHIPS.

BRUNSWICK DOCK WAS
BUILT IN 1789 AS THE FIRST
DEDICATED CARGO DOCK IN
LONDON, AND LATER
INCORPORATED INTO EAST
INDIA DOCK. THE TALL MAST
HOUSE STANDS AT ITS HEAD.

was removed in 1862, was the mast house, a tall building with a loft overhanging the river, under which unmasted hulls were floated to have their masts fitted. In 1789 the owner of the yard, John Perry, built Brunswick Dock, possibly the first purpose-built cargo dock in London: it was later incorporated into the East India Docks.

In 1612, the year the Blackwall yard opened, a Royal Charter was granted to the shipwrights of Rotherhithe, to build 'ships, carvels, hoys, pinnaces, ketches, lighters, boats, barges and wherries'. Rotherhithe's biggest yard was Randall and Brent's, second only to Blackwall for the supply of warships in the Napoleonic wars and cargo ships for the all-powerful East India Company. Randall and Brent's headquarters was at the Nelson Dock House – the only eighteenth-century house still standing in Rotherhithe Street, now a hotel. The influence of shipbuilders in Rotherhithe is apparent from the early eighteenth-century restoration of its parish church, St Mary's. Some of the pillars are made of timber, like masts, and the barrel roof was constructed very like a ship. Up river at Lambeth were smaller yards that specialized in building ceremonial barges, including those for the monarchs.

The advent of steam power brought big contracts to many Thames-side yards. The early paddle steamer *British Queen* was built at Curling and Young's at Limehouse. The most famous of all ships built on the Thames was the *Great Eastern*, designed by the engineer Isambard Kingdom Brunel and by far the biggest vessel of its time. This was laid out on the Isle of Dogs at John Scot Russell's yard. It was 629 feet long – too big to fit on to a conventional slipway – so it was built sideways on to the water. All the same, when the day came for its scheduled launch, it could not be shifted and there was a delay of several months before it was finally eased into the river. Part of the special slipway built for it is still in place, and can be seen alongside a new housing complex at Burrell's Wharf.

The introduction of iron hulls on freighters signalled the beginning of decline for the London yards. Significantly the very first iron ship, the *Aaron Manby*, was initially built in Birmingham in sections, which were despatched to Rotherhithe to be assembled. The London yards had already begun to be used for breaking ships as well as building them. The old wooden warship the *Téméraire* was being towed to Rotherhithe to be broken when Turner painted his evocative picture of her in 1838.

Other industries dependent on shipping grew up around the yards. Ropes and sails were made in Limehouse, Shadwell and Bermondsey, the ropeworks notable for their long covered 'walks', still marked on today's street maps, where the fibres were laid out flat and twisted together. Chain, wire and brass foundries were located in Bermondsey, Millwall and elsewhere. Although the shipbuilders were initially their main customers, they supplied other industries: ropes, for example, were widely used in coal mining.

BRUNEL'S GIANT STEAMER
THE GREAT EASTERN, BUILT
AT MILLWALL IN 1859.

Industries unconnected with the maritime trades also came to the Thames. Southwark was a centre of weaving from earliest times: the wool came by sea from East Anglia and the finished cloth was a lucrative export. Rocque's 1746 map shows nine 'tenter grounds' near the river, where the cloth was stretched after weaving. The advent of steam power transformed manufacturing processes in the nineteenth century and greatly increased the demand for coal. It meant that a riverside site would be the most convenient for virtually any form of industry, because coal could be unloaded direct from the ships. By the time electric and gas power became common late in the century, obviating the need for direct coal deliveries in many cases, the factories were already established and disinclined to move.

The new energy sources spawned industrial structures of their own. Large gasworks were erected at Greenwich, Beckton, Westminster, Wandsworth and Fulham. In 1889 the first high-voltage power station in the world was opened by Ferranti's at Deptford. Others soon followed – at Battersea, Fulham and

Bankside. In many cases their useful life lasted less than a century.

The shipyards had their own sawmills, but riverside timber yards supplied wood to the furniture and cooperage trades. The furniture workshops themselves were generally small-scale affairs located slightly away from the river in the East and West Ends. Bulky pianos were made at factories in Lambeth and at Millbank, Westminster – an area of light industry, slums and a notorious prison before it was transformed by the building of the Tate Gallery in 1897. Beer barrels came from cooperages close to the riverside breweries, while wooden casks for wine, herrings, tobacco, salt and other commodities were made and repaired by coopers who worked by the quays and docks and did not finally disappear until the 1960s.

STEELYARD WHARF, TYPICAL
OF THE STRING OF WHARVES
ALONG UPPER THAMES
STREET IN THE CITY,
PORTRAYED BY T.H.
SHEPHERD IN 1856. IT IS
NOW THE SITE OF CANNON
STREET STATION.

Building materials for the construction booms of the eighteenth and nineteenth centuries were often delivered direct or, in the case of bricks, actually made on the building sites, but if stone needed to be worked, the river was the only sensible place to do it. There was a large marble works in Horseferry Road in Westminster, and Eleanor Coade's artificial stone, adorning many notable London buildings, was made between 1769 and 1840 in a yard in Lambeth where the former County Hall is today. A lion made of the material stands guard, appropriately, on the building's western flank: it originally adorned the Red Lion brewery, next to the Coade stone works.

Ceramics on a more domestic scale constituted one of the longest-established industries on the Thames. Slipware tiles and vessels were made by small-scale artisans throughout the Middle Ages, and in the sixteenth century two Dutch potters came to London to make tin-glazed earthenware, or Delftware. After starting in the City they moved to Southwark, because the clay they used had to be shipped from Norfolk and Kent. Soon a string of

Delftware potteries was established along the river a little further west, between Lambeth Palace and the manor of Vauxhall. Salt-glazed stoneware, tougher but less decorative than Delftware, was also made here and across the river in Fulham, where part of the factory in New King's Road survived until the 1970s.

When the secret of porcelain manufacture was discovered, in the eighteenth century, factories were set up at Chelsea and Bow, as well as a less prominent one in Limehouse, whose existence has only recently been confirmed by archaeological excavation. Back in Lambeth, Doulton's pottery on the Albert Embankment became famous for its Art Nouveau designs as well as for its ubiquitous stone sinks, lavatories and urinals, until 1956, when production was switched to the Potteries, in Staffordshire.

Vauxhall and Southwark were also important centres for glass-making, using sand shipped in from Norfolk and the Isle of Wight. In the early sixteenth century the reputation of the Southwark School of Glaziers, just downstream from London Bridge, was so high that it won the commission for the stained glass at King's College Chapel in Cambridge: it would have been transported by river and sea, for it would certainly have broken if taken along the ill-made roads. Glass-makers seem to have been the hermit crabs of industry in the next two hundred years, establishing themselves in abandoned buildings such as Winchester Palace on the south bank and the Savoy Palace on the north.

Down river from Southwark, arriving sailors would brace themselves for a series of evil smells. Ink and dye were made from the seventeenth century at Deptford, with its deposits of copperas, the iron salt from which the products were made. In 1856 synthetic dye, made from coal tar, was developed at Shadwell, where Bergers had begun making paint in 1760. Bermondsey was for nearly three hundred years the headquarters of the most noxious of the riverside industries, leather tanning. At least thirty tanneries once existed in a small area centred on an impressive leather market, with covered colonnades surrounding an open courtyard. That has disappeared and the imposing Victorian Leather, Hyde and Wool Exchange is now unoccupied. Only a handful of the firms remain, but the street names – Tanner Street, Leathermarket Street, Morocco Street – bear witness to the trade that used to dominate the area.

GUSTAV DORÉ VIVIDLY PORTRAYED SLUMS OCCUPIED BY DOCKERS AND SEAMEN.

Ample supplies of water are needed for leather processing, so it was essential to be near the river, as well as being convenient for bringing hides and whole carcasses by ship from all over the world. Animal skins and furs were also used in the manufacture of hats, another industry that settled in Bermondsey.

Perhaps on the principle that one strong-smelling industrial process will blot out another, a vinegar factory was established near the Bermondsey tanneries and survived there until 1991. Vinegar is another long-established south London product. Beaufoy's had a production facility by the river in the eighteenth century until it was forced to move for the construction of Waterloo Bridge and went upstream to south Lambeth, where sweet British wines and vinegar were made until the 1960s.

Alcoholic beverages have long been a staple product of Southwark. London gin, the scourge of Victorian society, was distilled here and at other riverside locations, including Pimlico. Brewing is one of the oldest Thames-side industries. In Chaucer's *Canterbury Tales*, the miller cautioned:

> And if the words get muddled in my tale,
> Just put it down to too much Southwark ale.

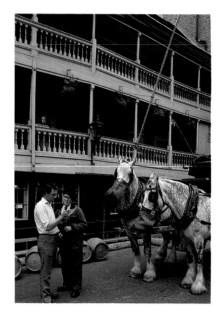

THE GEORGE, LONDON'S ONLY SURVIVING GALLERIED INN, WAS ONE OF NUMEROUS HOSTELRIES IN SOUTHWARK SERVED BY A CLUSTER OF BREWERIES ALONG THE SOUTH BANK OF THE RIVER.

Barclay and Perkins's Brewery stood next to the Anchor inn, just south of Southwark Bridge, near the site of Shakespeare's Globe Theatre, from the seventeenth century or earlier until 1982. The Anchor, which remains a favourite riverside inn, was for many years run in conjunction with the brewery, as an outlet for its products. In the eighteenth century the brewery belonged to Henry Thrale, a friend of Dr Samuel Johnson, while Mrs Thrale ran the inn. Boswell records that after Thrale died in 1781, Dr Johnson went to the auction sale of the brewery and stressed what a profitable business it was by telling a potential bidder: 'We are not here to sell a parcel of boilers and vats, but the potentiality of growing rich beyond the dreams of avarice'.

The Thrale brewery was bought at the auction for £130,000 by Robert Barclay, whose name was attached to its notable ale until it was taken over in 1955 by Courage, whose own brewery was a little up river in Rotherhithe, by Tower Bridge. Both have now been demolished. There were other breweries in Lambeth and, north of the river, in Limehouse and Mile End. Upstream were Young's in Wandsworth, Fuller's at Chiswick and Watney's at Mortlake.

Southwark was the clearing-house for one of beer's main ingredients, hops. They came from abroad as well as from Kent and the West Midlands, and were stored in large warehouses by the river. The Hop Exchange, built in Southwark Street in 1866, is now an office building, but its iron gates, decorated with hop designs, are still there.

Some of the food industries owed their foundations to the maritime trade. Ships' biscuits, a staple food for long voyages, were made in Rotherhithe, where Peek Frean's had a large factory. Jacob's were also in Southwark. Their ingredients were close at hand, for flour was milled at water and tide mills along the river. (Hovis flour came from Battersea, McDougall's from the Isle of Dogs, and Spiller's still have a mill near the old Royal Docks.) Sugar was refined at Ratcliff – between Limehouse and Wapping – and later further inland at Whitechapel. That led to sugar-based industries, particularly confectionery, being established in the East End, close to the docks.

Less than a century later, apart from one or two sugar and flour mills, scarcely any of these vigorous industries remain. Railways and roads provided faster transport and allowed modern factories to be built in hitherto undeveloped areas. It was fitting that the automotive industries themselves should set the pace for the move away from the river. Some started there: the first Vauxhall cars were made in Vauxhall, and Short's, the aircraft manufacturers, began at Battersea. (An even earlier industry connected with overland transport, the manufacture of horseshoes, thrived for a while on the Isle of Dogs.) But with the exception of Ford's, who still produce their cars and lorries by the Thames at Dagenham, the automotive industries quickly moved to the Midlands and beyond, closer to the source of their raw materials.

SIR GILES GILBERT SCOTT'S BATTERSEA POWER STATION, COMPLETED IN 1935.

Other heavy industries did the same. For a while Greenwich was the headquarters of the new science of electrical engineering, with Ferranti and Siemens establishing themselves there; but they too departed. The metal workers Morgan Crucible abandoned their factory, south of Battersea Bridge, in the 1970s.

After four centuries, industry was at last leaving the Thames. If this was bad economic news for the communities that surrounded the factories, for the river itself it meant the start of a long process of rehabilitation. When systematic pollution ceased, steps could be taken to clean it up and to bring fish and other wildlife back to areas from which they had been excluded for centuries. Then the banks themselves could be cleared, the factories and warehouses replaced by congenial dwellings; the modern equivalents of the medieval palaces, but on a diminished, more egalitarian scale. The end of one era is, by definition, the start of a new one.

CHAPTER SIX

BOATS AND SHIPS

*The Thames,
from London
Bridge to
Greenwich, I can
only compare to
an immense
moving street of
ships, large and
small, something
suggestive to the
Parisian mind of
an aquatic Rue
de Rivoli.*

EMILE ZOLA, 1899

PREVIOUS PAGES WILLIAM
JAMES'S PAINTING OF YORK
STEPS IN THE MID-18TH
CENTURY SHOWS THE
VARIETY OF SKIFFS,
WHERRIES AND SMALL
CARGO BOATS THAT
CROWDED THE RIVER ABOVE
LONDON BRIDGE.

FIRST THERE were primitive rafts and coracles, then Roman cargo ships with their square linen sails, colourful Viking boats with fearsome prows, ornate barges for princes and bishops, nimble wherries, fast sailing clippers, giant steamships, oil tankers and, today, river buses and police launches that dodge busily up, down and across the stream. Through its history the Thames has seen examples of nearly every type of boat constructed, including some designed specifically to cope with its peculiarities.

The first boats on the river were rafts made of logs lashed together with leather thongs. They were for carrying heavy weights and proceeded at no more than walking pace, since they had to be towed from the bank (like canal barges, but by humans rather than horses) or propelled with a single pole, like punts. Then came small canoes, dug out from tree trunks using primitive stone or early metal tools. Most journeys would be made partly on the river and partly on foot, depending on which provided the easier going: so the canoes had to be designed to be carried on the traveller's back. Because the wooden ones were excessively heavy they were replaced by boats covered with hide stretched over a light-weight frame. These were called coracles and were eventually made bigger to accommodate more than one person, as well as freight. They appear to have been a British invention, to judge from the observations of Avienus, a Roman travel writer in the sixth century BC:

> They have no art of building ships with pine and maple, or the tall fir, as most men do. Instead they curve the frame – and here's the marvel of it – with sewn skins they fit the craft and sail the high seas in a shell of hide.

(He was being unfair to English shipbuilders, for some pre-Roman wooden ships have been found elsewhere in the country, although not in the Thames.)

The coracles' rounded shape made them difficult to steer and to handle in high winds or a strong tide. Ocean-going boats needed keels to deal with current, as the Romans, with their long tradition of shipbuilding, knew. The earliest wooden ships whose remains have been found in the Thames are certainly Roman. The large barge excavated at Blackfriars in 1962 was 55 feet long and 22 feet across, its timbers joined with nails: later they were to use mortise and tenon wood joints. The caulking in the Blackfriars barge – the infilling between the boards to prevent leaks – was done with hazel twigs. It had a flat bottom so that it could negotiate the shallow Thames and was steered by a single oar at the back, rather than a rudder. It had a mast step used as a towing point when the sail was not up. The boat found on the site of County Hall in 1910 was of broadly similar construction.

The boats that used the river developed into two types; flat-bottomed barges for the upstream trade, and those with keels that plied the coasts and battled the open seas. The Viking long-ship, clinker-built (with overlapping planks), with a square sail, no deck, a high prow and stern – both coming to a slender point – set the pattern for ocean-going ships for centuries. Its immediate successor was the *knorr*, with a single deck. The Venetians meanwhile were building a large three-masted version, a galley. The addition of extra decks and an enclosed hold produced a ship suitable both for trade and for warfare, with a capacity of between 500 and 1,000 tons. It was steered by a rudder fixed to the stern, which necessitated cutting the stern away flat, distinguishing it from the pointed bow. These were called carracks or galleons – the latter term generally reserved for the fighting version – and their distinctive shape, with great expanses of sail and forecastles resembling medieval battlements, is familiar from contemporary pictures. They were the kind of ships that Henry VIII built for his navy.

Such giant vessels were rare visitors to the Thames compared with the smaller caravels which handled the coastal trade. Some 70 feet long with a single deck, they would sometimes have up to four masts, but without the great expanse of sail that the heavier boats needed.

Boats that went regularly up river had flat bottoms, so that the water would not be too shallow for them no matter what the state of the tide. Two types of flat-bottomed barge were developed for work in the Thames – one for the estuary and the coastal waters, the other to ply the non-tidal river above London. The estuary barges, called hoys (a term later used more specifically for passenger services from Margate), were sturdy and rode comparatively

THE UNION YACHT OFF BATTERSEA IN 1750, BY THOMAS PRIEST.

high in the water, so that they could cope with quite heavy seas. They derived from the plump Roman barges found on the river bed, many of whose features survived until the last Thames barges were built in the nineteenth century. Numerous barges were being made for work throughout Europe, each slightly different, to cope with the conditions of the river they were built for.

The Thames barges were swim-headed – in other words the flat bow was cut away at an acute angle to let the barge glide more smoothly in the water. At the stern was a long, heavy but necessarily shallow rudder. They would have one massive mast and usually a smaller one at the bow, and would carry a spritsail on a spar that rose diagonally from near the base of the main mast. The sails were a gingery brown – the colour of the preserving agent used on them – and were designed to give the maximum possible motive power consistent with limiting the crew to two, accommodated in a small cabin at the stern. Thames barges were in common use until well into the twentieth century and a few are still to be seen on the river, some adapted for seamanship training. There is one in the collection of historic ships at St Katharine Dock. Dutch *schuyts*, similar but squatter and used for eel fishing, were once a common sight but stopped coming after the Second World War.

For up-river work, a distinctive line of barges was developed, called western barges because they operated only west of London Bridge. They were narrow, flat-bottomed and up to 128 feet in length, with a maximum capacity of 170 tons and a draught of four feet. The largest of them were really too big for some locks and had to shed loads on to smaller boats to get through. A more convenient version was 88 feet long, carrying about 100 tons. Barges up to 17 feet wide could go as far as Oxford, but beyond that 11ft 9in was the maximum width.

Western barges were built mainly of oak, but many had elm bottoms. There was a mast which could be lowered to allow clearance beneath low bridges. A single square-rigged sail, again usually reddish-brown, would be set in suitable conditions: the more sophisticated fore-and-aft rig, with a spritsail, was not introduced until the nineteenth century. The mast was also used as a support for towing – in the early days by gangs of men (up to eighty of them for the biggest barges) and by horses after the eighteenth century. Long oars on board provided a third choice of motive power, and set-poles, up to 19 feet long, could be used for punting if necessary.

The western barges usually had no decks but often an awning overhead to protect the freight and – a secondary consideration – the crew. Their cargoes up river were grain, flour, cement, timber, bricks and many kinds of manufactured goods; on the way down to London they would often be carrying hay, vast quantities of which were needed to feed the capital's horses. In the eighteenth and nineteenth centuries the Thames was connected to the canal systems of the Midlands and West Country. Then the narrower boats conceived for canal work, brightly painted and with living accommodation, would be seen in the river. They are still common on its upper reaches, but used for recreation rather than work.

YACHTS OF THE CUMBERLAND FLEET IN THE LATE 18TH CENTURY, STARTING A RACE IN CHOPPY WATERS BELOW THE NEWLY-BUILT BLACKFRIARS BRIDGE, THEN KNOWN AS PITT BRIDGE.

A LIGHTER ENTERS
REGENT'S CANAL AT
LIMEHOUSE IN 1825,
BY T.H. SHEPHERD.

Taking coal up river was generally left to the larger vessels. Carrying coal had always been a specialized business and, although it was sometimes transhipped on to Thames barges, more often it would remain in the sturdy colliers that had brought it from Newcastle. When power stations were built up river from London, the colliers were redesigned so that they would sit low enough in the water to negotiate the bridges. They were nicknamed 'flatties' and, although they no longer work the river, a few are still moored in it.

The other working boat commonly seen was the lighter, or 'dumb barge', which operated in the harbour to ferry goods from ship to shore. In the seventeenth century, with trade so brisk that most ships could not count on being able to tie up by the quays, there was a demand for a basic workhorse to ply to and fro, ferrying the cargoes. Lighters originally moved around the harbour using the tides – of which the lightermen needed detailed knowledge – and a single 25-foot oar for steering. With the coming of steam they were often pulled by tugs.

Lighters survived as long as the docks. In his 1966 book *The Thames*, A. P. Herbert wrote:

Those ugly black swim-headed 'dumb' barges, with no motive power of their own, are the lowly cousins of the graceful sailing barge, now dead. They play a great part still in the trade of the port and their wooden ancestors, of whom a few remain, were at the heart of it. . . . It does not sound very modern or remarkable, a single man in charge of a vessel which has no engine of its own. Yet this ancient partnership is found economical and efficient, even in the Jet Age.

The demand for lighters grew rapidly as, after the first enclosed docks opened at the start of the nineteenth century, ever larger vessels began to come up the river, serving the expanding trade with the Empire and the Americas. Steam dredgers, mounted with untidy but practical digging machinery, became a familiar sight as the riverside wharves, too, were adapted for the bulkier ships. The dredgers' present-day successors are prominent among the comparatively few vessels seen on the Thames today.

The first steam-powered ships appeared on the river in 1815, but steam and sail coexisted for a surprisingly long time. As Romola and R. C. Anderson point out in their book *The Sailing Ship*, the introduction of steam at first led to the building of bigger and faster sailing ships, because the advent of steam-powered tugs meant that they did not have to worry so much about being manoeuvrable in port. For most of the nineteenth century an immense variety of sailing ships could be seen on London's river. Contemporary paintings and, later, photographs show the Pool of London as a crowded forest of masts and sails, as evocatively described by Emile Zola in the quotation that begins this chapter.

IN 1865 THE LINER TANCORE WAS ONE OF THE LAST LARGE SHIPS BUILT IN LONDON.

In the eighteenth century the East India Company had a monopoly of trade with the east and it was thus the only company operating the large ships required for the routes. When restrictions on foreign ships were lifted in 1849, new types of vessel came to the Thames, in particular the clippers, the fastest large sailing ships. These slender schooners were first built in Baltimore in the 1830s. The speed of the clippers was especially valuable for the Chinese and Indian tea trade, because tea deteriorates if stored in a ship too long. The best-known British clipper is the *Cutty Sark*, built in Dumbarton in 1869 and now on display at Greenwich. It is striking for its economy both of line and of interior fitments: essentially it is nearly all storage space, a floating warehouse with no frivolous aids to comfort that could impair its performance. The crew were sparsely provided for.

Ironically, in the year that saw the launch of the *Cutty Sark* came a development that began the decline of merchant sailing ships. The Suez Canal was opened, which meant that steamships could now travel to the Far East without going round the Cape of Good Hope – then impracticable for steamers because it involved a journey of some five thousand miles between coaling stations, as against two thousand miles through the Canal. The sailing ships survived longest on the long Australian run, where wool was the chief commodity. They were still being built in the twentieth century: the six-masted *Wyoming*, the longest wooden sailing ship ever, was launched in 1910, and the five-masted *France* three years later. But these had auxiliary engines for use when the wind was uncooperative: the days of sail were numbered.

The clippers and the large sailing ships increasingly catered for passengers. Until the middle of the nineteenth century there were no large ocean-going vessels built specifically for carrying people, because there was

insufficient demand. Long-distance overseas travel was comparatively rare. The only passengers travelling in bulk were slaves, who could be carried in the hold like any other freight. The few paying passengers could be accommodated in cabins close to the crew's quarters.

Mass migration from Europe to North America and Australasia changed that. Because of the large numbers who suddenly wanted to travel, ships were adapted to cater for them. The clippers initially dominated this trade because they were the fastest boats on the seas, and the passengers did not want to be subjected to the inconvenience and discomforts of ocean travel for any longer than was absolutely necessary.

With steam and later diesel came the construction of large ocean liners, but London never developed into a major port for them. Southampton was less than two hours away by train and the vast natural harbour of Southampton Water, with its freak tidal pattern which causes high water to come more frequently, was relatively uncluttered by freight traffic. The journey by 'boat train' was successfully marketed as a pleasurable part of the voyage. Many of the early transatlantic emigrants came from Ireland, which meant that Liverpool, with the initial advantage of being on the west coast, was much more convenient. Tilbury, 24 miles east of London, just opposite Gravesend, was developed as London's main passenger port, and some ocean liners would start there before calling in at Southampton: but after a while they found it not worth the detour. In an attempt to lure them back, an elaborate passenger terminal, with a fast rail link to St Pancras, was built at Tilbury in 1957; but within a decade nearly all inter-continental passenger traffic had been captured by jet aircraft.

By contrast, carrying short-haul passengers has always been integral to London's river life. With only one bridge, passenger services across the river, as well as up and down it, were for years as important as those for freight. On short trips, passengers were conveyed by watermen in skiffs and wherries, light and slender boats propelled by an oarsman or sculler, taking as few as two or as many as eight passengers either straight from one bank to the other, or a few miles in either direction. Those who wanted to cross with horses and carriages had little choice: if they did not want to brave the congested bridge, they had to use the horse ferry from Westminster to Lambeth, recalled in the name of Horseferry Road in Westminster.

For longer river journeys there were, from medieval times, public services, operated on a schedule that in those early days depended on the tides. From Roman times there was possibly a service from Gravesend in Kent to Billingsgate, the 'Long Ferry', covering a distance of some twenty miles. It is referred to in a medieval document of 1293, when the fare was a halfpenny for a trip in one direction. By 1370 it was up to twopence – a level at which it appears to have been maintained for some two centuries. In the early sixteenth century the trip took four hours and the spritsail-rigged barges were limited to carrying 24 passengers, although they soon grew in capacity. Smaller and faster vessels called tilt-boats, because they were covered with a tilt or awning, also plied the route and quickly became popular. By 1595 tilt-boats, now powered by five oarsmen plus the sails, were authorized to carry up to thirty passengers, and within forty years the maximum had increased to forty. Service on the Long Ferry was maintained until well into the nineteenth century, after the introduction of steamboats.

Another old-established service to London operated from Margate, using the distinctive square-rigged Margate hoys, carrying up to seventy passengers plus freight on a journey which could take anything from eight to 48 hours, depending on the weather and tide. Bunks were available in communal cabins, and if the boat was full they were hired on the basis of occupation by three alternating passengers. The hoys began offering on-board entertainment in the nineteenth century but were soon superseded by the faster and more convenient steamboats. Closer to London, there were ferries from Erith and Woolwich, where today's free car ferry, established in its present form in 1889, has antecedents going back at least seven hundred years.

The first paddle steamers went into service on the Thames in 1815, taking passengers upstream to Richmond and downstream to Gravesend and Margate. They were notable for their immensely tall funnels, which had to be folded down towards the deck at bridges. The first boat, the *Margery*, had a 30-foot funnel which doubled as a mast, suggesting that the builders were not entirely confident in the new technology. Mechanical breakdowns were indeed common in the early days, and it was several years before the public was sufficiently persuaded of the reliability of steam to abandon sailing ships entirely. Later the funnels were reduced in size, and sometimes a second one was added, while screw propellers gradually replaced paddles as the driving force.

In the second quarter of the nineteenth century the steamers enjoyed great prosperity, being popular with commuters as well as for weekend river excursions to the seaside and to the newly-opened Rosherville Pleasure Gardens near Gravesend. The traffic was not regulated, and the steamboat owners would use the traditional cajolery of the watermen to lure passengers on to the unsightly and ramshackle piers that they had constructed themselves. The brisk business brought fierce competition and price-cutting, and several steamship companies failed or were taken over. By 1850 the boom times were gone: the faster railways took most of the commuter traffic, and the Thames boats concentrated more and more on leisure trade. The boats grew bigger and bigger until they could accommodate several hundred trippers. One of the largest, the paddle steamer *Princess Alice*, was involved in the river's worst accident in 1878, when it was mown down by a collier on the way back from a trip to Sheerness and 640 people were drowned.

By the end of the century the roads and railways into London were becoming congested and an attempt was made to revive river commuting. In 1905 the London County Council instituted a frequent river bus service between Greenwich and Hammersmith, but it now had a powerful new competitor in the trams. The LCC river bus could never attract anything like enough passengers, especially in winter, and it lasted only three years. The fleet of boats bought for £200,000 was sold for £18,000, London ratepayers taking the loss. After the Second World War river buses were revived, and received a fillip from the Festival of Britain in 1951, but closed down in 1962. Only in the late 1980s, with the development of offices in the abandoned docks, did a commuter service become a viable proposition once again.

For most of the twentieth century, then, river passenger traffic has primarily served the recreational market. Cruises to the seaside towns on the estuary, and even across the Channel to Boulogne, were popular until the Second World War, but suffered from a change in leisure patterns. First the cinema and then television made increasing claims on people's time and, more significantly, the great upsurge in overseas travel meant that a mere cruise down the river and back seemed tame and unsophisticated. In 1966 the last two boats making trips from London to Southend, Margate and the Channel ports were withdrawn.

But the increase in tourism was a world-wide phenomenon, and London's river services adapted to cater for it. The fleet of modern boats making short

A STEAM TUG TOWS A BARGE ABOVE ALBERT BRIDGE, CHELSEA, IN 1890.

river trips from Westminster Pier expanded to meet the demands of visitors. There are sightseeing trips up river to Richmond, Kew and Hampton Court and down river to the Tower, Greenwich and the Thames Barrier. Growing use is made of the boats in the evenings, too, when they have become popular for private parties and corporate entertaining. One of the attractions of a river boat, especially for young people, is that loud music can be enjoyed without disturbing neighbours. Stand on one of the capital's bridges on a summer night and you will first hear and then see a succession of boats parading slowly past, with music blaring, strobe lights flashing and writhing dancers silhouetted against the windows.

Enjoyment of the river takes many forms. Its most glamorous boats for many centuries were the ornamental state barges, used for carrying royalty and other dignitaries on formal occasions and processions and sometimes on routine river trips. These opulently carved and decorated barges, constructed as greatly enlarged wherries, would be rowed by perhaps two dozen oarsmen wearing bright livery. Apart from royal occasions, the most spectacular annual event on the river was the Lord Mayor's Show, which took place on water from the early fifteenth century until the City of London ceded control of the Thames in 1857. Apart from the mayor's barge itself, the most important City livery companies built their own, each vying with the others to be the most splendid, hung with colourful awnings, banners and heraldic devices. As new bridges came to be built from the eighteenth century onwards, the barges would be brought on to the river for the opening ceremonies.

One of the most moving of the large river pageants took place in 1806, when Lord Nelson's body was taken up river from Greenwich in a royal barge originally built for Charles II. In 1849, when Prince Albert headed a river procession to open the Coal Exchange near Billingsgate, he rode in Queen Mary's shallop, built in 1689. In 1912 King George V and Queen Mary used the same barge to visit Henley Regatta and again for the peace pageant on the Thames in 1919. It is now on display, with other ceremonial barges, at the National Maritime Museum in Greenwich.

The purpose of state barges is to impress spectators by symbolizing the monarch's wealth and power. The same role is played today on a more mundane level by the dumpy private motor yachts, or 'gin palaces', fitted out in so luxurious a style that the owner's guests are apparently supposed to forget they are on the water at all. A less pleasant way of symbolizing power is with a show of force, which is why warships have been seen regularly in the capital's waters throughout history, ever since Henry VIII took to building them in Deptford. They serve no military purpose in the river, for not since the Vikings has anyone seriously attempted to launch a full-scale invasion up the Thames estuary; yet they have always been welcome visitors, inspiring awe as the crew of a frigate line the deck and salute while passing through the raised roadway of Tower Bridge. Ships of the Royal Navy and from friendly foreign navies still visit London, and the Second World War cruiser *HMS Belfast* is there permanently, moored opposite the Tower and open to visitors.

A FLOTILLA OF SMALL BOATS ACCOMPANIES LORD NELSON'S COFFIN ON ITS PROCESSION TO ST PAUL'S CATHEDRAL FOR HIS FUNERAL IN 1806. ON THE LEFT ARE THE ADELPHI TERRACES.

CHAPTER SEVEN

TRADE AND THE EMPIRE

Along the quay
you see, now men
with their faces
blue with indigo,
and now gaugers
with their long
brass-tipped rules
dripping with
spirit from the
cask they have
been probing.

HENRY MAYHEW, 1861

THE WEST India Dock, London's first, opened for business in the northern section of the Isle of Dogs on 27 August 1802. Enclosed behind a high wall and with its private police force, it was so successful in keeping out the plunderers who had plagued the wharves for years, that other shipping companies were persuaded to seek similar protection. Three years later the London Dock opened at Wapping and the following year the East India Docks at Blackwall, based on the Brunswick ship repair dock that had been there since 1789. The East India Company's ships had been especially prone to cargo robbers since the West India Dock opened.

In 1820 the Regent's Canal Dock opened at Limehouse, providing a direct link to the Midlands through the canal system, and in 1828 the most westerly of the great docks, St Katherine, was built, at the cost of destroying an important hospital and thousands of homes. Later in the century came the Royal Victoria and Royal Albert Docks, east of the Isle of Dogs, and Millwall Dock, on the southern part of the Isle. On the south bank were the Surrey Docks in Rotherhithe, for years the centre of London's timber trade.

These enclosed docks sparked a revolution in the port's commercial pattern and created extensive new riverside settlements, especially in the hitherto undeveloped Isle of Dogs. This was a marshy expanse, used for cattle grazing and milling, which had, at its southern tip, the landing-point for the long-established ferry from Greenwich, which Samuel Pepys occasionally used. In her *Outline History of the Isle of Dogs*, Eve Hostettler writes:

> With the docks and shipyards the island's first industrial population appeared, to excavate the docks and build the warehouses, then to operate the dock system. There were clerks, coopers, lock-keepers, dock police, engineers, warehousemen, carters, stable-boys, smiths, porters, stevedores and dockers. Amongst the women were laundresses, street-sellers, beer-house keepers, shirt-makers, needlewomen and nurses.

The fields were quickly covered with small terraced houses to accommodate the influx of new workers and their families, who came from all parts of Britain. The builder William Cubitt opened a yard on the west of the Isle and built a model housing estate, Cubitt Town, for its workers. (He was the younger brother of the more famous Thomas Cubitt, who was responsible for many of the stucco terraces of Belgravia, Pimlico and Bloomsbury.) By the middle of the century, some fifteen thousand people were working on the Isle, and the number increased when Millwall Dock was constructed in 1868. A speculative enterprise which was opened to exploit the new trade expected following the repeal of the Corn Laws, Millwall specialized in handling grain, and a number of flour millers, notably McDougall's, set up plants there, providing further jobs.

The warehouses in the new docks and the older wharves were not simply used for trans-shipment but were lively centres of commerce in themselves,

PREVIOUS PAGES THE WEST
INDIA DOCK AND ITS
WAREHOUSES, ON THE
NORTH OF THE ISLE OF
DOGS, SHOWN IN 1802, WHEN
THEY WERE BUILT TO
ACCOMMODATE THE
GROWING EMPIRE TRADE.

where commodities were unpacked and prepared for sale. Tea was sampled and blended in the warehouses, where the different types of leaf were heaped on the floor and mixed together with wooden spades. Wool and silk were weighed, the wool baled and graded and sold direct from the warehouses at regular auctions. Timber was sorted and stacked. Decorative items such as ivory, shells and exotic feathers were laid out on the floor for buyers to inspect.

Yet despite all this colourful activity the docks prospered only spasmodically. Although they had superlative deep-water facilities, they could never offer the convenience of the riverside wharfs, and it was correctly assumed that not many shipping companies would choose to use them unless compelled to. So the first three docks were granted 21-year monopolies for the import of specific items.

Goods from the East and West Indies had to be unloaded in the docks named after them, while tobacco, rice, wine and brandy had to go to the London Dock. At the same time the system of imposing customs duties was formalized. When ships reached Gravesend, customs officers would board and lock the holds containing dutiable items. These could be unlocked only in the presence of customs agents, who would supervise the unloading of the goods

WEST INDIA DOCKS: SHIPS DECKED FOR THE OPENING CEREMONY.

into bonded warehouses at the new docks. Duty would be payable only when they were taken ashore from the warehouses.

This still left the old legal quays to handle commodities such as hides, grain and some fruit, which came from Europe in smaller ships. Because of the increase in the general level of trade, the quays continued to be profitable and their business grew again when the docks' 21-year monopoly expired. Under the legislation which established them, the docks were obliged to let lighters move in and out free of any charges. This so-called 'free water clause' meant that ships could enter the docks and unload their goods on to lighters, which would then take them out to more convenient riverside wharves, where storage costs were usually lower. The practice deprived the docks of much of the warehousing business on which their profits depended, and was among the reasons why they began to fall into financial difficulties soon after their monopoly privileges ended. Despite rationalization – the East India and West India companies merged in 1838, and London and St Katherine in 1864 – the docks had reached a parlous condition before the end of the century.

Fluctuation in trade meant uncertain prospects for the dock workers. A few had permanent jobs as dockers, who unloaded ships, and rather more as stevedores, who loaded them. The stevedores were the aristocrats of the docks, for loading required more skill and experience than unloading and attracted higher pay. Below the permanent workers in the dock hierarchy were the 'preference men', guaranteed a certain number of days' work a year. The majority, though, did not even enjoy that level of security. They were hired on a casual basis by the day, half-day or even by the hour. They would be required to turn up early in the morning or at midday at one of the hiring points, usually just outside the dock gates, where they would clamour for work either from the dock employers themselves or from contractors commissioned by the docks to supply labour for them. Henry Mayhew wrote in *London Labour and the London Poor:*

> It is a sight to sadden the most callous, to see thousands of men struggling for only one day's hire . . . For weeks many have gone there and gone through the same struggle, the same cries; and have gone away, after all, without the work they had screamed for.

The arrival of ships was erratic, dependent upon seasonal and other factors. Fruit, sugar and timber, for example, only arrived at certain times of the year. One week up to two hundred ships might enter a dock, the next week no more than thirty. This insecure and unpredictable routine contributed to the instability and hardship rife in the East End in the second half of the nineteenth century. Mayhew maintained that it was responsible for much of the drunkenness, because if men were not hired they would repair to one of

ABOVE GUSTAV DORÉ'S DRAWING DEPICTS THE OFTEN DANGEROUS PROCESS OF LOADING AND UNLOADING GOODS AT THE TALL WAREHOUSES THAT LINED THE WHARVES.

LEFT DIGGING OUT ST. KATHERINE DOCK, BELOW THE TOWER, IN 1828.

the scores of pubs clustered round the dock gate. The constant uncertainty, combined with the low rates of hourly pay, made the dock labour force responsive to the incipient trade union movement. The tea warehousemen at West India Dock were the first to become organized and took part in small strikes there in 1871 and 1872. In 1886 Ben Tillett emerged as a powerful spokesman and was among the leaders of a dispute at the newly opened dock at Tilbury. He became general secretary of the tea warehousemen and spread their influence throughout the docks. Three years later Tillett and John Burns were the driving forces behind Britain's first major dock strike, which shut down the dockyards for a month.

The demand was for the dockers' tanner, an hourly rate of sixpence (2½p) instead of the prevailing fivepence and fourpence. As in many of the landmark industrial disputes of the time, the strikers won a wide measure of support, fuelled by press reports, such as Mayhew's, of the dreadful living conditions that prevailed in the East End. Each day of the strike the dockers would march through the City to show their solidarity and were joined by other port workers such as shipwrights, sailors, lightermen and watermen in their traditional livery. Cash donations from the public and from workers overseas strengthened the men's resolve.

A conciliation committee was established that included the Bishop of London and the Roman Catholic Cardinal Manning. In response to its recommendations the employers capitulated and granted the sixpenny rate, with eightpence an hour for night work and a minimum total payment for any work of two shillings (10p). After the strike the Dock, Wharf, Riverside and General Labourers Union was formed to protect the gains that had been made, with Tillett as its general secretary. Because of the publicity attracted by the strike, Tillett and his dockers became a powerful element in the emerging trade union movement in Britain.

As far as the employers were concerned, their defeat in the strike increased the already mounting financial pressures on them. With the undoubted social benefits of trade unionism came its corresponding drawbacks. The men, growing in confidence, increasingly used their industrial muscle to pursue grievances, not always in all-out strikes but in local stoppages and, more often, deliberate slowing-down of the work. As delays mounted, the dock owners agreed to allow shippers to hire their own labour. This worsened the effects of casualization, because it meant that there were now numerous employers, each having his own 'call' every morning. Choosing the place to seek work now became more of a lottery than ever. A man might go to one point and fail to catch the eye of the recruiter, while not far away more jobs were being offered than there were men to fill them.

JOHN BURNS ADDRESSES STRIKERS AT WEST INDIA DOCK IN 1889.

There were other problems for the docks. Oddly, the imperial expansion and the introduction of large steam freighters in the last quarter of the nineteenth century did not cause the upsurge in business that had been expected. In particular, the opening of the Suez Canal did not herald the hoped-for boom, because many shippers now chose to unload their goods from the Far East at Mediterranean ports rather than continue to Britain. For sure, there were quantities of exotic silks and spices to be seen on the London quaysides and in the warehouses – Mayhew used them to point a contrast with the impoverished daily life of the workers – but they did not arrive in the quantities needed to ensure prosperity for the enclosed docks.

Moreover, the growth of industry in the north meant that many cargoes now went in and out of Liverpool, Manchester, Newcastle, Glasgow and Hull. In London, improvement and enlargement of the riverside wharves meant that shippers were increasingly taking advantage of the 'free water clause' by unloading their goods on to lighters inside the docks and taking them outside for warehousing. Most important, the channel from Gravesend into London was not deep enough for the new larger ships, some of which had to unload

THE 1828 OPENING CEREMONY OF ST KATHERINE DOCK, THE NEAREST ENCLOSED DOCK TO CENTRAL LONDON. THOUSANDS WERE MADE HOMELESS WHEN THEIR HOUSES WERE DEMOLISHED TO MAKE WAY FOR IT.

part of their cargo downstream in order to rise high enough in the water to get through.

The dock companies competed for what business there was by investing in new facilities and cutting their profit margins to the bone. When the London and St Katherine group decided to build the Royal Albert Dock, their rivals at the East and West India docks invested in extensive new facilities at Tilbury, 26 miles towards the estuary, with fast rail links to central London. But the steamship companies preferred the more central docks, and the East and West India company were forced to lure ships in by slashing their charges. The rival group then had to match the cuts in order to keep business in its own new dock.

By 1888, just two years after Tilbury opened, the East and West India company was in receivership and was forced to combine its operations with those of its competitor. In 1901 the two groups were formally merged and eight years later, after a Royal Commission report, control of all the London docks was transferred to a public body, the Port of London Authority, and £22m paid in compensation to the former owners.

Under their new ownership, the docks at last began to prosper in the years leading up to the First World War, and even managed to win a victory over their workers. In 1910 the dockers' union had been absorbed into the larger Transport Workers' Federation, the precursor of today's Transport and General Workers' Union. There was a brief strike the following year, resulting in a further penny an hour on the pay, and a larger and more bitter stoppage in 1912, in which the union demanded a closed shop. The employers retaliated by hiring non-union labour to replace the strikers, and the union had to accept defeat.

By 1913 the port was handling more than 20 million tons of cargoes, worth over £400m a year, which represented about a third of all trade passing through British ports. The tonnage had quadrupled since the 1850s and was ten times higher than at the beginning of the nineteenth century. More modern facilities were built as the ambitious development plan, although interrupted by the war, continued to be pursued after it. Muirhead's *Blue Guide to London and its Environs*, published in 1918, describes it thus:

> London's position as a great entrepot of trade, through which pours an unceasing and colossal stream of wares of every kind, invests its docks with a variety and interest unequalled elsewhere. No one can view without interest the spacious basins crowded with shipping of every flag discharging cargoes from every region between the poles and equator, the huge warehouses for the storage of goods, the apparatus and machinery adapted for every need, or the constant skilled activity that prevails. A long day's visit to the docks is fatiguing; but a visit should be paid at least to London Docks. Luncheon, if required, should be brought; the eating-houses and taverns near the docks are not adapted for the ordinary visitor.

Nobody doubted that the prosperous commerce thus described would be maintained and increased. What was to be the last dock in the system was opened in 1921, the King George V Dock, immediately south of the Royal Albert Dock in Silvertown. This new facility could handle ships of up to 30,000 tons and was used by the huge liner *Mauretania*, although not regularly: the big passenger liners remained reluctant to base themselves in the Thames. In his *History of the Port of London*, published in the year the King George opened, Sir Joseph Broodbank wrote:

> The future of the Port of London is as secure as the future of any human institution can be. Even though the British Empire should have been disintegrated and despoiled as a result of the late struggle it is impossible to believe that the Port of London, with its natural

BUILDING WOODEN SHIPS AT LIMEHOUSE IN THE MID-19TH CENTURY.

advantages enhanced by the expenditure of many millions on facilities, would have ceased to occupy its pre-eminent position as a market or distributing centre. But with the triumph of the Allied forces and the extension of the Empire's power and influence, we have the prospect of increased commercial operations in the chief port of the Empire, and as a consequence an augmentation of shipping and merchandise there which should, as the years proceed, bring an increment of trade to the Port enormously beyond anything that has hitherto been dreamed of.

In the event, such prosperity as there was never lasted long enough to produce any marked effect on the living conditions of the people who worked at the docks and lived in the neighbourhood. The 1918 *Blue Guide* describes the parts of Stepney close to the river – Limehouse, Shadwell and Ratcliff - as 'a region of poor streets inhabited largely by a "marine" population'. Charitable efforts to alleviate the poverty and its consequences, by such Victorian institutions as the Salvation Army, Dr Barnardo's Homes and Toynbee Hall, could only nibble at the edges of the problem. One of the worst afflicted areas was that round Cable Street, mainly the preserve of Irish labourers and known as Knockfergus.

SEAMEN FROM ALL PARTS OF THE WORLD BROUGHT EXOTIC VICES TO THE AREAS OF THE EAST END ADJACENT TO THE DOCKS, AS IN THIS IMAGINATIVE 1885 DEPICTION OF AN OPIUM DEN.

Many foreign seamen decided to stay, forming small enclosed ethnic groups of Chinese, Malays, West Indians and Indians (known as Lascars). Limehouse became London's first Chinatown and the venue for the capital's first Chinese and Indian restaurants. For a while, in Victorian times, it attracted sightseers, drawn by the unusual food as well as by tales of opium and gambling dens, sailors' bars and other mysteries; but they were soon deterred by reports of attacks on strangers by the variety of villains who congregated in the crowded, lawless streets around the docks. Jack the Ripper, who murdered prostitutes in the Whitechapel area in 1888, also helped to fuel the East End's sinister reputation.

The need to improve matters was universally recognized but, before much could be done, economic circumstances again conspired against it. In the years immediately after the First World War the tonnage handled in the docks doubled in quantity, but the worldwide slump that began in 1929 had a dramatically damaging impact on trade, and Britain was at the same time losing its domination of international merchant shipping. Revival was slow and was halted by the Second World War, when the Thames estuary was mined and most of the docks and their warehouses were destroyed by bombs.

The worst raids were on the morning and night of 7 September 1940, when four hundred German bombers systematically sought to destroy the entire dock complex. Fires raged through warehouses, feeding on inflammable products such as spirits, sugar, coal, textiles and timber. The timber yards at Greenland Dock in Rotherhithe were still smouldering a week after the raid. The bombs that fell in that 24-hour period killed 430 dockside residents and workers. The Woolwich ferry ran all night to evacuate people from Silvertown to the south side of the river.

Yet the attack, though devastating, was not completely successful. The docks remained in use for military and civil purposes throughout the war, albeit on a much reduced scale. The war also saw a significant improvement in the employment conditions of dock workers, inspired by Ernest Bevin when Minister of Labour. Bevin introduced the National Dock Labour Board, which paid dockers a guaranteed minimum wage whether there was work for them or not, over and above the payments received when they actually worked.

When peace came the Port of London Authority invested more than a million pounds in rebuilding and modernizing dock facilities. Oil refineries and tank farms were built, and oil soon became the most important single product handled. (Today, small oil carriers serving the riverside power stations are among the working boats seen most often on the Thames.) In 1964, cargo amounting to 61,339,000 tons passed through the Port of London; a figure that was never to be exceeded. In 1970 the long tradition of casual labour in the docks was abolished altogether and all workers were paid a fixed weekly wage.

THE POOL OF LONDON DURING NIGHT RAIDS BY GERMAN BOMBERS IN 1941.

Despite these changes, the docklands communities remained a world apart and, to outsiders, something of a mysterious and unwelcoming one. This was partly because their geography cut them off from the rest of London.

Residents of the Isle of Dogs were separated from Limehouse by swing bridges and dock gates which barred traffic when ships passed through. It was the same across the river in Rotherhithe: many families lived in insanitary housing in 'Downtown', the name they gave to the cluster of damp, narrow alleys off Rotherhithe Street, which hugged the river bank while behind it was the great expanse of the Surrey Commercial Docks, isolating it from Bermondsey and Southwark. Public transport was sparse and slow, adding to the alienation but also fostering a strong collective spirit.

The people's working and social lives centred on the river, marking them out from those with the mundane preoccupations of dry land. The welter of dockland reminiscences that have been recorded in recent years, in print and on film, identify a people who, at least in retrospect, were proud of the hard conditions of their everyday lives and mourn the sense of common purpose that these conditions inspired. The swiftness of the destruction of the docks and their supporting communities in the 1970s made the sense of loss even harder to bear.

CHAPTER EIGHT

DECLINE AND REBIRTH

*There will always
be a port of some
kind in the
Thames. But
whether in twenty
years it will be
the insignificant
relic of long years
of idleness,
inertia and
waste, or whether
it will be a major
port still based on
Tilbury but with
thriving terminals
along the
riverside, is
largely up to us.*

PORT OF LONDON
AUTHORITY INFORMATION
PAPER, 1978

PREVIOUS PAGES BY 1972,
WHEN THIS PICTURE WAS
TAKEN AT LIMEHOUSE, FEW
LARGE SHIPS WERE TO BE
SEEN IN THIS PART OF THE
RIVER, BECAUSE OF
CHANGING PATTERNS OF
TRADE.

LONDON'S LIFE as a major international port ended with astonishing suddenness. In 1967, only a few years after the peak traffic year, the East India Dock was closed. A year later London and St Katherine Docks went, and in 1970 the Surrey Commercial Dock, already partly filled in, discharged its last ship. At the same time the riverside wharves closed one by one, causing a collapse of the lighterage business. A study group formed by the Department of the Environment and the Greater London Council predicted in 1973 that by 1988 all the enclosed docks above Tilbury would be redundant. They underestimated the speed of events; for in 1982 the King George V Dock, the last to be built, became the last in the London area to shut down.

Two changes in techniques for carrying freight during the 1960s started the headlong, irreversible decline. From being the most convenient place to load and unload, the capital swiftly became the most inconvenient. First, on long sea voyages, goods were transported in giant containers, usually packed at inland depots and designed to be loaded intact on to flatbed trucks and then hauled by road to their final destination. Second, produce from Europe was now increasingly carried on the roll-on roll-off Channel ferries, on which the containers did not even have to be detached from the lorry cabs. The first requirement for a container or a roll-on roll-off port is that it should provide easy access to the motorway network, and this was decidedly not an attribute of the congested streets around London's docks. Moreover, container ships are larger than old-style freighters, and therefore harder to manoeuvre in the river. Once a good container port had been constructed at Tilbury, there was no incentive for ships to go further upstream.

Another factor in the collapse of business was the new deal for dock workers. This led to lower productivity, causing delays in loading and unloading that persuaded more shippers to seek alternative havens. The problem was partly alleviated by the introduction of a bonus system for dockers, but by then the damage had been done.

As more docks closed there were far too many registered dock workers. Some moved to Tilbury – technically part of the London docks system and under the control of the Port of London Authority, but 26 miles from the City and even further away in spirit. Lord Aldington, chairman of the PLA, said that in 1976 about £150,000 a week was being paid to London dockers for whom no work was available. The need to offer attractive redundancy payments increased the economic difficulties of the remaining yards.

It was never going to be easy to find a use for more than five thousand acres of abandoned docks, nearly half of it filled with water. The first, comparatively modest redevelopment came at St Katherine, the most westerly of the docks, just below Tower Bridge on the north bank. In 1969, less than a year after the dock closed, work began to convert its eighteenth-century warehouses and nineteenth-century dock buildings into a complex of offices, a hotel, shops, restaurants and a marina. Just a five-minute walk from the Tower and Tower Bridge, two of London's busiest tourist attractions, the complex could scarcely fail to draw visitors itself, and now receives more than two million a year, who come to look at the historic ships on show, do their shopping and eat in the restaurants. (These include the Dickens Inn, housed in the shell of an eighteenth-century warehouse moved a few hundred yards from its original site.) The shops, hotels, restaurants and offices in St Katherine Dock provide employment for some five thousand people.

Initially, it was natural that the sites nearest the City should be the easiest to put to alternative uses. In 1978 Rupert Murdoch, the forward-looking newspaper proprietor, became convinced that the days of Fleet Street, as the main production base for Britain's national newspapers, were numbered, because neighbouring property was too expensive for expansion and the streets too crowded for convenient access. Seeking a new site to print the *Sun* and *News of the World*, he found it just east of St Katherine Dock on part of the old London Docks at Wapping. There he built and equipped a large printing plant and had plenty of space left over for editorial and administrative offices and for subsequent expansion.

A pointer to the down-market reputation of Wapping in the 1970s came in the initial decision of Murdoch and his executives to identify the plant as being in Tower Hamlets, which they thought sounded more dignified. But popular usage triumphed and Wapping not only regained its identity but became inscribed in newspaper history after Murdoch moved all four of his papers there (by then he had *The Times* and *Sunday Times* as well) in January 1986. He had left the plant empty for some three years while he tried in vain to negotiate staffing arrangements with the print unions, but finally he made the move using workers from other unions, thus beginning a swift revolution in the labour practices and production techniques of national newspapers. For nearly a year regular demonstrations took place outside the Wapping plant – to the annoyance of local residents – but the print unions failed to win back their former status.

MANY OF THESE STURDY VICTORIAN WAREHOUSES, WHICH LINED BOTH SIDES OF THE RIVER EAST OF TOWER BRIDGE, HAVE BEEN CONVERTED INTO LUXURY APARTMENTS.

The appearance of Wapping and the demonstrations on television news on a regular basis was not in itself good publicity for the new Docklands, but in the longer term it did help bring to people's attention the constructive aspects of the changes in train there. Progress on redeveloping this and the other Docklands areas had been slow throughout the 1970s. There had been residential developments in Wapping and Rotherhithe, mainly involving the conversion of old warehouses into spacious apartments with dramatic river views. A handful of optimistic members of the middle class moved into the few presentable riverside houses in Wapping and Limehouse that had not been razed for warehouses years ago.

Most prominent of the pioneers was David Owen, at that time a rising star on the Labour front bench, and his American wife Debbie, then Jeffrey Archer's literary agent. They bought a house in Narrow Street, Limehouse, near the Grapes, one of the half-dozen historic riverside pubs that have survived. Among their neighbours were Michael Barraclough, a doctor, and his wife Jenny, a television producer. The Barracloughs saw the possibilities for residential development in the Isle of Dogs, a place of mystery for most Londoners, where twelve thousand council tenants lived, surrounded by a few small factories and the remains of the West India and Millwall Docks, both about to follow their neighbours into disuse.

Exploring the southern tip of the Isle in the early 1970s, Jenny found a boiler works with a breathtaking view across to Greenwich and the National Maritime Museum (Wren's former naval hospital). The couple negotiated to buy the site, and three couples agreed to join them. They built themselves a short terrace, easily recognizable from the river because of their high, pointed roofs, like sails. The remaining land on the site has since been developed by a housing association and Wates, one of the large private house-builders.

For the most part, though, commercial and residential development in Docklands languished in the decade after the first docks closed. During the 1970s successive governments appointed committees and consultants in an attempt to evolve a plan for this enormous area of derelict land which clearly had the potential, given the right infrastructure, of resuming its former strategic and economic importance to the capital.

In 1979 the new Conservative Government and its Environment Secretary Michael Heseltine devised a formula for development that encapsulated its philosophy of the state being a facilitator of private enterprise instead of going into business on its own account. The London Docklands Development Corporation (LDDC), established in 1981, was charged with acquiring all the land in the area already in the public sector – mainly owned by the PLA, British Rail and local councils – and preparing it for development and sale. To get things moving quickly, the corporation took over from local councils the role of planning authority in its areas, angering councillors who pointed out that it was an appointed and not an elected body. The LDDC was envisaged as a body with limited life, devoted to getting development under way and disappearing from the scene in a dozen years or so.

Most of Docklands was declared a development area, qualifying for incentives that included generous capital allowances and a ten-year freedom from property taxes between 1982 and 1992. While that concession was only of short-term advantage, the capital allowances would enable developers to supply modern office space at significantly lower rents than those prevailing in the City and the West End. Starting with nearly eight hundred acres in and around the Isle of Dogs, the LDDC quickly acquired another four hundred acres in Surrey Docks on the south side and a further six hundred when the Royal Docks closed a few months after the corporation was established. Under the legislation, the land had to be bought at existing use values, which were low since most of it was redundant. Acquisition costs ranged from £3,000 to £40,000 an acre, with between £30,000 and £40,000 an acre being spent on preparation and infrastructure.

The lack of transport links that had given Docklands its special character became a liability when development was planned. Road construction began

immediately but could never provide the complete solution to the problem of conveying thousands of people to work every day in the new offices that were envisaged.

The first major scheme to fill the gap was completed in July 1987, when the Queen opened the Docklands Light Railway, an elevated line initially able to carry 1,750 passengers an hour from the southern tip of the Isle of Dogs to Tower Hill to the west and Stratford to the north.

IN THE EARLY 1980S THE OLD MILLWALL DOCKS ON THE ISLE OF DOGS LAY DESOLATE AND ABANDONED. BY THE END OF THE DECADE THEY WOULD BE REVITALISED BY NEW DEVELOPMENTS.

The railway offers views over Shadwell, Limehouse, the old West India Dock and the Isle of Dogs, where, by the late 1980s, the brightly-coloured cranes and barges laden with steel, stone and cement provided evidence of the pace and scale of redevelopment. Such was the demand for this new rail service that the decision was made to enlarge it to carry 6,500 passengers an hour, and to extend it westwards to Bank underground station, where it will connect with the tube network. There are also plans to extend the overhead railway eastwards to Beckton and southwards across the river to Greenwich and Lewisham. In a few years the Isle of Dogs will get its first underground station when the Jubilee Line is extended to Canary Wharf, passing through Rotherhithe on its route.

Three months after the opening of the Docklands Light Railway, the London City Airport came into use, built on landfill between the old Royal Albert and King George V Docks. Its runway is not designed to accommodate large jets, but there is a regular scheduled service of STOL (short take-off and landing) passenger aircraft to Paris, Brussels and Amsterdam. There are plans to extend its runway and increase its range to central and southern Europe and traffic is expected to grow as the major developments in the Docklands area are completed.

SUNSET OVER DOCKLANDS, WHERE THE ONCE BUSY RIVER IS DESERTED.

One way of travelling to the airport is by river bus. The 62-seater catamarans, augmented in 1990 by three larger and faster models, provide scheduled services between the West End, the City, the Isle of Dogs and Greenwich and serve the airport every half hour. The main service runs every twenty minutes for commuters from the south whose trains arrive at Charing Cross, Waterloo, London Bridge and Cannon Street. There is also a service between Charing Cross and Chelsea Harbour.

Following the example of Rupert Murdoch, other newspapers planning their retreat from Fleet Street also looked eastwards to the Docklands area. It was a fortunate coincidence, so far as the LDDC was concerned, that the break with traditional newspaper production methods came at a time when its first Dockland sites were available for development. Proprietors saw that the earlier they could move in, the greater would be the benefit of the no-rates concession. The *Daily Telegraph* group acquired a 17-acre site for a new print works by the old Millwall Dock in the Isle of Dogs, and when it was clear that they had over-estimated the capacity they needed, they sold a half-share to the *Express* group. After the Canadian Conrad Black gained control of the *Telegraph* group he decided to move its editorial office as well as its print works out of Fleet Street and rented space in the new Isle of Dogs development at South Quay, less than a mile from the printing plant. Soon the *Telegraph's* editorial office will move to the skyscraper at Canary Wharf.

Other newspaper owners decided against putting their editorial people in

Docklands, but found it ideal for their new high-tech print works. *The Guardian* and the *Financial Times* built plants in the Isle of Dogs, the *Daily Mail* group in Rotherhithe, and the news agency Reuters set up an office for its financial information services in the old East India Docks, right by the river. Northern and Shell, the magazine publishers were one of the first large companies to go to the Isle of Dogs. Banks, restaurants, shops and office equipment dealers moved in to supply the needs of the new businesses.

Already, then, a useful commercial enclave was being established close to the centre of the Isle, but despite the transport improvements it was still perceived as a quaint and slightly inconvenient outpost of the City. It needed a more substantial focal point to make it into a viable community in its own

SHIPS IN THE OLD MILLWALL DOCKS FRAME THE BUILDINGS OF SOUTH QUAY PLAZA.

right. The mid-1980s was marked by a strong surge of economic activity which created a corresponding surge in the demand for office space in central London. Also during this period there were changes in the way stock trading and financial business was conducted in the City – the so-called 'big-bang'. It meant that overseas banks and other financial services institutions needed greatly to expand their London operations. These two factors created an unprecedented demand for modern office space which could not be met in the City and West End without severe disruption. The LDDC, in co-operation with the Canadian developers Olympia and York, conceived a large alternative financial centre at Canary Wharf, at the northern end of the Isle. Dominated by a 50-storey skyscraper, the 71-acre site, described in the final chapter, is being developed to provide twelve million square feet of office space and supporting services, with the first tenants moving in during 1991.

The success of this scheme will shift the centre of gravity of the city's commercial district eastwards. This will have a knock-on effect on the whole of

Docklands, especially on the many acres of empty land surrounding the old Royal Docks in the Beckton area. Three major schemes for development, involving a mix of offices, shopping, housing and entertainment, faltered because of the slump that began to affect the economy in 1989. When economic conditions improve and Canary Wharf is fully operational, there is little doubt that the Royals, in their turn, can be developed successfully.

In the 1980s large-scale house-builders also moved into Docklands. In the mid-1970s, shortly after the Barracloughs and their friends took their pioneering initiative on the southern tip of the Isle of Dogs, Bovis put up a small close of houses in Capstan Square, on the Isle's north-western edge. They sold well and attracted the attention of journalists, who portrayed the residents as the advance guard of the middle class in a traditional working-class area. Other large house-building groups followed the lead, and by the mid-1980s most of the riverside sites were filled with housing in occupation or under construction.

Further east at the Royal Docks, and on the south bank in Rotherhithe, housing took precedence over commerce. In Rotherhithe and Bermondsey, dozens of acres of abandoned wharves were cleared of their industrial buildings, and part of the former Surrey Docks was filled in to provide new space for housing, with supporting shopping facilities and access roads. The filling of the docks did much to end the inaccessibility of the Downtown area – the community centred on Rotherhithe Street – but it was not universally welcomed. The kind of housing to be built, and for whom, was the subject of impassioned disputes between the existing local residents, the LDDC and the developers.

It was not that the residents opposed all change. They certainly did not want the abandoned warehouses to remain, providing shelter for a large population of rats. The issue was how much of the new housing should be in the public sector, for existing poorly-housed residents, and how much for the luxury market, for sale to the prosperous middle class. The new housing in Rotherhithe and elsewhere is a mixture of private and public schemes, many of the latter managed by non-profit housing associations.

While developments in Docklands made the headlines, because of their scale and their ambitious nature, things were also happening upstream. Chelsea, long associated with art and style, was never going to be as difficult to market to prospective residential and commercial tenants as the mysterious expanses of the East End. The old railway goods yard alongside Chelsea Creek, west of Lots Road and Cheyne Walk, has become Chelsea Harbour, 18 acres of costly apartments, offices, shops, restaurants and an all-suite hotel, with views across to St Mary's Church in the old village of Battersea – a favourite subject with the artists who inhabited Chelsea in the nineteenth century. At the centre of the development is the former Chelsea Dock, now a 75-berth marina, and alongside that the Belvedere, a 20-storey skyscraper with a single luxury apartment on each floor, the higher ones offering views up and down the river and across central London. A golden ball on top of its

pyramid-shaped roof rises and falls to indicate the level of the river. Between the city centre and Chelsea are smaller housing developments on either side of the river. Crown Reach on the Pimlico side of Vauxhall Bridge faces some stark new red-brick flats on Nine Elms Lane, while south of Battersea Bridge a 1980s housing estate stands on the site of the former Morgan Crucible factory. Downstream from Battersea Park the old power station, with a stately white chimney at each corner, may one day become the centrepiece of a large-scale amusement park.

Londoners have always exploited their river: for trade, defence, industry, communications, health and today as a visual and leisure amenity. But it has been no easy conquest. The Thames has a dynamic and sometimes dangerous life of its own. It must be harnessed and tamed and constantly overseen to prevent its running out of control. The next chapter shows how, down the centuries, this task has been attempted.

MATURE TREES LINE WEST INDIA AVENUE LINKING CABOT SQUARE WITH THE GARDENS AT WESTFERRY CIRCUS AND THE RIVERSIDE PROMENADE.

CHAPTER NINE

TAMING THE RIVER

I do not know

much about gods;

but I think that

the river

Is a strong brown

god – sullen,

untamed and

intractable,

Patient to some

degree, as at first

recognized as a

frontier;

Useful,

untrustworthy, as

a conveyor of

commerce;

Then only a

problem

confronting the

builder of

bridges.

T.S. ELIOT, *THE DRY
SALVAGES*, 1941

To a city, a river is like a passionate but difficult lover: indispensable, yet uncomfortable to have around. Until the Romans came, the Thames had its own way with London. It was a formidable barrier. Those who wished to cross it without a boat would do so at the brown god's convenience, when the tide was right, and would usually undergo a soaking for their temerity. Archaeologists suggest that the river was more easily fordable when the Romans came than it was a thousand years later. They speculate that its level may have risen substantially in Saxon times, since when it has not been fordable at Lambeth or Brentford, formerly viable crossings.

It is impossible to say how often the old wooden London Bridge was replaced before its stone successor was completed in 1209. Wooden piles discovered on the crossing site prove that the Romans built a bridge, but it was poorly maintained after they left and may have fallen into disuse from time to time. Against wood, however sturdy when installed, a fast-flowing river will always ultimately get the upper hand. Contemporary references indicate that a bridge stood in the tenth century, but what was there in the preceding five hundred years is uncertain.

A curate, Peter of Colechurch, was put in charge of building the first stone bridge in 1176, and he was dead before it was completed. His remains, buried in the bridge's structure, were discovered when it was eventually demolished in 1824, but were not preserved. Old London Bridge is best known for the houses that stood on it until the eighteenth century, and for the heads of traitors that were displayed on its southern entrance, but it was its structural peculiarities that had the greatest impact on the river. The bridge, 300 yards long and 13 yards wide, rested on nineteen piers forming pointed arches. Between two of the piers the bridge could be raised to let ships pass. Because the arches were narrow and the piers massive, the bridge's effect on the flow of the river was as disruptive as that of a partial dam. Water would rush in and out of the narrow gaps (creating, as we have seen, a hazard for boatmen), while above the bridge the tidal action was restricted, allowing the river to freeze in the coldest winters, when 'frost fairs' would be held on the ice.

Yet there it was, a colossal piece of medieval engineering, and there it stayed, despite its defects, for more than six hundred years. For most of that time it was the only land crossing in the London area. It was crowded, rumbustious and a focal point of the capital's life. Lobbying by the powerful watermen meant that it kept its exclusive status far beyond the time when economic arguments – and simple considerations of convenience – demanded additional bridges. Not until the eighteenth century did local interests manage to force through plans for a second bridge, and that was at Putney, several miles upstream. The wooden bridge with 28 narrow openings, completed there in 1729, may not have done much in itself to ease the problems of Londoners, but it did set a precedent, and seven years later Parliament was persuaded to pass legislation allowing a bridge at Westminster.

The cost of the new bridge, met partly by the proceeds from a lottery, was increased by the need to pay compensation not just to the watermen but also to the Archbishop of Canterbury for loss of revenue from the horse ferry by Lambeth Palace, which he controlled. After delays caused by engineering problems the bridge was opened in 1750. It was immediately popular but not a long-term success. For one thing, the alcoves built on the road above the fifteen stone arches were colonized by prostitutes and brigands. More gravely, it suffered from structural weaknesses and had to be replaced after little more than a hundred years.

London Bridge was forced to adapt to meet the new competition. In 1760 the old houses, most by now shored up with wooden supports, were finally removed, which made room for an extra traffic lane and helped ease congestion. At the same time the centre arch was enlarged so that bigger boats could pass through without the swing mechanism having to be deployed, again reducing road delays. But now that a start had been made, more and more bridges were planned and built. In 1768 came Blackfriars Bridge, between London and Westminster Bridges, and afflicted like the latter with defects in its construction.

THE FIRST WESTMINSTER BRIDGE, JUST AFTER ITS COMPLETION IN 1750.

Before the end of the century, bridges had appeared at Battersea, at Richmond and at Kew, on the site of the old Brentford Ferry. In central London the next important development came in 1811, when work began on Vauxhall Bridge, giving access to the popular Vauxhall pleasure gardens and opening up areas of south London that had hitherto been largely undeveloped, but which could now accommodate part of the capital's swiftly increasing population. Vauxhall Bridge, briefly known as Regent's Bridge, was the first of the Thames bridges to be made of iron. It was opened to traffic in 1816, one year before the opening of the Strand Bridge, later called Waterloo Bridge to commemorate Wellington's victory over Napoleon in 1815. Southwark Bridge was opened in 1819, provocatively close to old London Bridge, which by now was starting to show its age by comparison with the modern (though sometimes less well built) rivals that challenged it.

John Rennie, who had designed both Waterloo and Southwark Bridges, was one of the main advocates of pulling down the old stone London Bridge and replacing it with one better adapted to modern needs. He died before the scheme was approved, but his son, also called John, supervised the completion of the new bridge, which opened in 1831. With only five arches compared with the former nineteen, the new Bridge had a liberating effect on the tidal river, allowing a freer flow of water above it. This meant the end of the frost fairs – the last was in 1814 – and also caused damage to some of the bridges upstream, which had not been designed to withstand the more rapid current. Blackfriars and Battersea Bridges were particularly affected and soon had to be

ABOVE BLACKFRIARS BRIDGE, BUILT IN 1768, WAS A POPULAR ALTERNATIVE TO LONDON BRIDGE FOR TRAVELLERS AND FOR THE SOUTHWARK BREWERS TAKING THEIR BEER TO THE CITY.

RIGHT THE GREAT FROST FAIR OF 1739-40, BY GRIFFIER.

replaced. Indeed during the late nineteenth and early twentieth centuries all the older road bridges in the London area were rebuilt to cope with greatly increased traffic loads as well as with the faster flow of the river. The abolition of tolls on all bridges in 1879 (celebrated in a ceremonial drive across five of them by the Prince and Princess of Wales) helped to reduce road delays but inevitably increased the use of the bridges, and thus their wear and tear. Even three built in the second half of the nineteenth century, at Chelsea, Lambeth and Wandsworth, were replaced in the 1930s. Nor was Rennie's Waterloo Bridge immune to the stresses of twentieth-century traffic, and in 1937 work started on Sir Giles Gilbert Scott's sleek new version, completed in 1944. The last surviving Rennie crossing, London Bridge, was dismantled and sold to a theme park in Arizona to make way for the new one that was opened in 1973.

That left Westminster Bridge (rebuilt in 1862) as the oldest surviving road bridge in London, ahead of the reconstructed Blackfriars (1869) and the attractive Albert Bridge, between Chelsea and Battersea, a suspension bridge erected in 1879 and saved from destruction only by two sturdy stone piers put

A MIXTURE OF STEAM AND
SAILING SHIPS CELEBRATE
THE 1894 OPENING
CEREMONY OF TOWER
BRIDGE. IT REMAINED THE
MOST EASTERLY THAMES
BRIDGE FOR NEARLY A
HUNDRED YEARS.

underneath it nearly a hundred years later. An earlier suspension bridge,
built at Hammersmith in 1827, had to be replaced in 1884.

The demand for bridges was effectively insatiable. Like all new roads,
their very existence encouraged people to use them, so they swiftly recreated
the congestion they were built to alleviate. In the 1870s the growth of the docks
led to calls for new crossings downstream from London Bridge. The problem
was how to accommodate the large ships accustomed to proceeding to the City.
The Corporation Bridge Committee considered many schemes to provide an
extra crossing and still let the ships through. Joseph Bazelgette's scheme for a
high-level bridge was rejected in favour of one by Horace Jones, the City
architect. He devised that stately monument to Victorian engineering and
imaginative architecture, Tower Bridge, with its high walkway (closed as a

regular pedestrian route in 1911) between towers and a road that opened skywards to allow the tall ships through. Its neo-Gothic appurtenances, designed to blend with the Tower of London, quickly made it into one of the city's most familiar landmarks and it is open to tourists, who can cross the upper walkway and inspect the imposing engines that used to power the lifting mechanism. Now electrically operated, the bridge is opened infrequently today.

By the middle of the nineteenth century it was not only road traffic that had to be conveyed across the river. The railways serving the growing southern suburbs and coastal resorts had to find ways of getting their trains into the heart of the city. (The single exception was the London and South-Western railway, which built its terminus first at Nine Elms, east of Battersea, then further east at the southern end of Waterloo Bridge.)

The first railway bridges were built in western London, at Richmond and Barnes in the 1840s. The Grosvenor Bridge from Battersea to Pimlico followed in 1860. The first to serve the City came in 1864, with a crossing into the new Cannon Street station and another alongside Blackfriars road bridge. In the same year a footbridge leading to Hungerford Market, near Trafalgar Square, which had been designed by Isambard Kingdom Brunel in 1845, was expanded to take rail traffic into Charing Cross. In 1886 a second rail bridge was built at Blackfriars, where the three bridges – two rail and one road – stood side by side until the earlier of the two rail bridges was demolished in 1984. The last rail bridge in London was constructed in 1889, to carry the District Line between Fulham and Putney.

The idea of a tunnel crossing beneath the river, avoiding any interference with shipping, had long been a seductive one, but again the river was not easy to tame and until the mid-nineteenth century the technology did not match up to the concept. In 1799, responding to a proposal by the engineer Ralph Dodd, Parliament approved a bill allowing a tunnel linking Tilbury and Gravesend, but flooding caused the digging to be abandoned in 1802. Three years later Richard Trevithick tried to construct a foot tunnel between Rotherhithe and Limehouse, but the flooding problem again proved insoluble.

ROBERT CRUIKSHANK'S
CARICATURE OF THE
TROUBLES BESETTING
BRUNEL'S TUNNEL.

The inventive Marc Isambard Brunel made the breakthrough when he developed the Great Shield, a tunnelling machine that enclosed the construction workers in an iron tube. As the tube moved on the tunnel was immediately lined with bricks behind it. In 1825 his men began work on a foot tunnel between Rotherhithe and Wapping. Despite the success of their invention, floods were not entirely eliminated and progress was slow. There were casualties among the work force, as well as difficulties from methane gas. In 1843 the tunnel was finally completed and a million people paid the twopenny toll to walk through it in the first fifteen weeks, patronizing the souvenir and refreshment stalls through its length. Brunel was knighted, but after the initial interest the tunnel was not much used, becoming a sink of vice and squalor. In 1870 it was converted into a railway tunnel, which it remains today.

In 1869 the Tower subway was built, connecting Tower Hill with Tooley Street, near London Bridge Station. People travelled through it in rope-hauled trams, but again, after initial success, the erection of Tower Bridge made it largely redundant. Further east, beyond the bridges, tunnels capable of accommodating wheeled traffic were eventually built, and survive today as an integral part of the capital's transport network. The first purpose-built tube tunnel, following the line of London Bridge, opened in 1890. The mile-long Blackwall road tunnel opened in 1896, the Rotherhithe Tunnel in 1908 and the Dartford Tunnel in 1963. A foot tunnel, taking dockers to work at Millwall, was built between Greenwich and the Isle of Dogs in 1902. A tunnel was sunk in 1906 to carry the Bakerloo Line from Charing Cross to Waterloo and another rail tunnel was constructed at Woolwich in 1913. The next planned river crossing will be the longest bridge across the Thames, carrying a new road across the river downstream from Docklands.

It was not just as an obstacle to overland travel that the Thames proved an inconvenience to the inhabitants of the city that it had spawned. In two important respects it was positively dangerous. By the nineteenth century the amount of human and industrial waste being poured into the river made it foul-smelling and insanitary; and from time to time a combination of perverse winds and high tides led to fatal flooding. In AD 48, even before London was established, many thousands of people are recorded as having drowned in a flood all along the river's length. There was another in 1099, and in 1236 boats were said to be plying the great hall of the Palace of Westminster. In 1555 Westminster Hall was flooded again, and in 1663 Pepys noted 'all Whitehall having been drowned'. Floods in 1764 meant that bargemen were unable to work for two months, and ten years later the bridge at Henley was swept away. The Duke of Wellington's funeral in 1852 was disrupted by unusually high water.

Floods eventually subside, but the effects of river pollution worsened with time. As early as 1357, Edward III was complaining about the 'dung and other filth' on the river banks exposed at low tide, and the 'fumes and other abominable stenches arising therefrom'. The Plague and the Black Death thrived under such insanitary conditions. Cholera epidemics in 1832, 1848 and 1849 struck hardest at people who lived near the Thames and its tributaries, where foul raw sewage would float past their back windows. At low tide the banks of the river were seen – and smelt – to be strewn with more and more filth, and during the Great Stink, in the summer of 1858, Members of

IN THE LATE 19TH CENTURY FLOODING OF THE THAMES GREW MORE FREQUENT. IN 1891 THE FLOODS REACHED AS FAR UP RIVER AS WINDSOR, AS SHOWN HERE IN THE *ILLUSTRATED LONDON NEWS*.

Parliament could scarcely tolerate the putrid atmosphere in their fine new building. In an attempt to cure it, large quantities of lime were thrown into the river, and even the curtains of the Houses of Parliament were soaked in a lime solution.

The experience of 1858, coupled with the campaigns of health advocates such as Edwin Chadwick and John Snow, prompted MPs that year to approve a plan drawn up by Sir Joseph Bazalgette, chief engineer of the Metropolitan Board of Works (forerunner of the London County Council) to build a sophisticated main sewer system that piped waste ten miles out to Barking Creek, and later directly into the sea and not the river. The main sewer pipes were built into the new Victoria, Albert and Chelsea Embankments, which channelled the river on its way through central London. On the north side, the embankments also housed the track for the new Circle Line railway which ringed central London, linking most of the main rail termini.

With tides getting higher by the year, the embankments proved an imperfect defence against flooding. Over the last century the tides measured at London Bridge have shown an average increase in height of 60 centimetres.

BY 1857 THERE WERE SIX BRIDGES BETWEEN WESTMINSTER AND THE TOWER.

THE INNOVATIVE THAMES
BARRIER AT WOOLWICH,
COMPLETED IN 1984 AT A
COST OF £500M, SHOULD
KEEP LONDON SAFE FROM
FLOODING UNTIL WELL INTO
THE 21ST CENTURY

This is part of a world-wide phenomenon caused by the melting of the polar ice-caps, which increases the volume of water in the oceans. In the case of the Thames, the effect is aggravated by the gradual south-east tilt in the British land mass.

The river has burst its banks several times since the embankments were constructed, notably in 1881, 1894 and 1928 – the last time central London was badly affected. (The disastrous east coast floods of 1953, which inundated Canvey Island, largely spared the capital.) Raising the height of the embankments and river walls was only a temporary palliative which could not be applied indefinitely. After many years of debate on how best to protect London from potentially devastating flooding, it was decided to build a retractable barrier near Woolwich. Co-ordinated by the Greater London Council, the work began in 1974 and the Thames Barrier, costing some £500m, was opened by the Queen ten years later.

The visible part of the barrier consists of seven helmet-like roofs above concrete piers housing the mechanism for operating the six D-shaped gates.

These rest on the bottom of the river, so as not to impede shipping. The gates are rotated upwards when a flood is threatened and, together with the four smaller overhead gates at the sides, form a wall six foot higher than the river rose in 1953. This should ensure London's safety for several decades but, with water levels continuing to rise, further preventative measures will eventually be required.

Well before men began seriously to tame the river, they were exploiting it for transport and for two necessities of life, water and fish. By the sixteenth century water towers and pumps had been set up by the river to provide water for domestic use, and it remained a prime – if increasingly polluted – source even after the New River was constructed in the seventeenth century to bring much cleaner spring water from Hertfordshire to the capital. Water companies began to introduce systems for filtering out impurities after campaigns by the same health lobbyists who had encouraged the construction of the sewer system. Filtering the water after extracting it from the river was of no help to the fish, which for years were unable to penetrate the filth beyond the lower reaches. Records speak of a variety of fish, including salmon, all along the Thames until the eighteenth century, and one persistent tale has it that medieval apprentices complained of a surfeit of salmon in their diet. Whitebait were also caught in profusion in the London area, while oysters, a popular and cheap dish, thrived on the mud flats at the river's mouth, near Colchester and Whitstable.

THE RIVER POLICE HAVE
PATROLLED THE THAMES
FOR MORE THAN 150 YEARS.

The fish gradually disappeared when the Industrial Revolution and its toxic wastes came to the river in Victorian times. Modern sewage disposal methods, together with the disappearance of most riverside industry, have greatly improved matters, and fish are once again to be seen – and occasionally caught – in the London area.

If the Thames itself had to be controlled, so too did the people who used it. With cargoes of immense value passing along the river daily, there were plenty of opportunities for theft. One contemporary estimate at the end of the eighteenth century was that as many as half the goods entering the port of London were destined to be stolen. High walls and strong gates on the docks deterred theft from the warehouses, but the only way to prevent cargoes disappearing mysteriously from ships was for an alert police force to patrol the river in boats. The West India Dock Company was the first to form its own water-borne police force, based on the same pier at Wapping that accommodates the modern headquarters of today's river police, who have operated since 1839 as an arm of the Metropolitan Police. With fewer ships to watch over, the river police now spend part of their time recovering the bodies of people who, by their volition or by accident, have become sacrificial offerings to the strong brown god.

Presently comes Creed, and he and I by water to Vauxhall, and there walked in Spring Garden. A great deal of company, and the weather and garden pleasant: that is very pleasant and cheap going thither, for a man may go to spend what he will, or nothing, all is one. But to hear the nightingale and other birds, and here fiddles, and there a harp, and here a Jew's trump, and here laughing, and there fine people walking, is mighty divertising.

SAMUEL PEPYS, 1667

THERE IS a sense of escapism about a river. It is a place where normal rules seem not wholly to apply. For sure, it has its own code of navigational practice, enforced rigorously for the sake of mutual survival. Perhaps because of these strict obligations and the privations of river life, watermen, like seamen, are granted more latitude than the rest of us when their behaviour comes to be judged. That spirit of tolerance extends to the river bank which, through London's history, has provided a haven for many of its racier pleasures.

The meticulous sixteenth-century chronicler John Stow was especially meticulous in researching the seamy side of life, and he traced what he called the 'bordello or stews' of Bankside back at least as far as the reign of Henry II in the twelfth century. A parliament then enacted rules for the conduct of brothels which, according to the ordinance, confirmed 'the old customs that had been there used time out of mind'.

The much-quoted rules laid down that the women should pay no more than fourteen pence a week for their rooms; no married women or women of religion should be accommodated; no diseased women should work there; no food or drink to be sold on the premises; no soliciting; no Sunday opening; and once having agreed the price with the customer, the woman must stay with him all night – perhaps the earliest stab at consumer protection.

Stow also discovered licences for Bankside brothels dating from the fourteenth and fifteenth centuries, and proclamations closing them for short periods. They were smashed up by Wat Tyler's rebels in 1381, but, in response to the unflagging demand, they quickly reopened. Henry VII had them closed in 1504 because of a syphilis epidemic – it may have been where his son Henry VIII caught it – but within a year the most persistent profession in the world was back in business, although some of the brothels began to be converted into taverns.

Even when used for their original purpose they were named like inns – the Cross Keys, the Cardinal's Hat, the Bell, the Boar's Head. Their signs were painted on the backs of houses, facing the river, so that they could be seen from the north bank. The women were colloquially known as 'Winchester Geese', no doubt because the brothels were close to the Bishop of Winchester's palace, and some of them in property that he owned. Any whore who transgressed could be accommodated conveniently in the Clink, the most famous of Southwark's five prisons and the first regularly to admit women.

Edward Alleyn, the founder of Dulwich College, owned many of the stews in the late sixteenth century and married into more when he wed the daughter of a rival whoremaster. In the seventeenth century the brothels began to languish and were banned during the Commonwealth, when some of the women were shipped to the new American colonies as wives for the settlers. The Great Plague of 1665 put paid to most of the Bankside pleasure houses, but not of course to the trade itself.

Stow also recorded two bear gardens on Bankside, used for the baiting of both bears and bulls by mastiff dogs, kept in kennels on the premises. The

PREVIOUS PAGES A CAMBRIDGE CREW TRAINS FOR THE UNIVERSITY BOAT RACE.

gardens were at first essentially plots of open ground surrounded by scaffolding for the spectators to climb on to, similar to early theatres - indeed so similar that Wenceslaus Hollar, in his famous panorama of London published in 1647, confused the Bear Garden with the Globe Theatre. Every Sunday in the sixteenth and seventeenth centuries up to three hundred people would go to watch the gory sport and gamble on the results, despite the disapproval of such as the diarists John Evelyn, who called it a 'rude and dirty pastime', and Samuel Pepys, for whom it was 'a very rude and nasty pleasure'.

Philip Howard, in his 1975 book *London's River*, provides a vivid description of bull-baiting:

> Bulls were generally matched with one highly trained and savage dog at a time. The bull was tethered by its horns to a stake with a rope about fifteen feet long. Owners stood around outside the perimeter of the rope holding their dogs by the ears, and releasing them to make their charges one at a time. The dog tried to dodge past the bull's defences and sink its teeth into vulnerable flesh. The bull warded it off with its feet and horns, which were cased in wooden sheaths for the benefit of the dogs. The bull tried to slip its horns beneath the dog and toss it high in the air to break its neck or back, if the spectators did not manage to catch it.

THOUSANDS LINE THE OLD BATTERSEA BRIDGE TO CHEER MISS YOUNG, ''THE FEMALE BLONDIN'', AS SHE WALKS A TIGHTROPE FROM BATTERSEA TO CREMORNE PLEASURE GARDENS IN CHELSEA.

Many spectators were crushed to death at a bull-baiting in the Paris Garden in 1583, when the balcony collapsed. The site of the Paris Garden is still marked by a street of that name south and west of Blackfriars Bridge, while further east there is a street called Bear Garden, by the Anchor tavern. Horse Shoe Alley, nearby, was the venue for bowling matches which provided another vehicle for gambling.

That these disreputable sports took place cheek by jowl with London's most popular theatres, and were patronized by largely the same audiences, helps us understand the raucous reputation of the seventeenth-century theatre, as compared to the more aesthetic connotations of the theatre today. The Rose, the Globe, the Hope (part of Alleyn's entertainment empire) and the Swan, venues for plays by Shakespeare and his contemporaries, were all established on Bankside in the late sixteenth and early seventeenth centuries.

The authorities of the City of London frowned on public entertainments of all kinds, because they encouraged gatherings of disorderly people. The first purpose-built theatres were established north of the City, in Clerkenwell and Shoreditch, in the 1570s. Soon the river exercised its lure and the theatre district moved to Southwark, with its tradition of illicit pleasures: indeed the bullrings themselves had hitherto occasionally been used by the players. In many of the world's cities, even today, one area accommodates both the red light district and the theatre district: in both, it could be said, artifice is employed for the enjoyment of the punters.

Taking a boat across the Thames to see the play added spice and adventure to a night out. The theatres themselves were flimsy, wooden structures with covered seating around a stage usually open to the elements. Performances could only take place on fine afternoons, and a flag would fly above the theatre on the day one was scheduled, so that potential customers in the City would not make a fruitless journey across the water.

One of the earliest playhouses in Shoreditch, called simply The Theatre, was taken down, transported south and re-erected on Bankside in 1599, to become the first Globe. This burned down and a replacement was built, a replica of which is today being constructed close to the original site. There was excitement among London historians in 1989 when the foundations of the Rose were discovered just upstream from Southwark Bridge, for this was the first hard archaeological evidence of the exact position of any of the early theatres.

Although Bankside saw the flowering of Elizabethan and Jacobean drama, its reign as the pre-eminent theatre district was brief. After the Restoration, playgoing became respectable and fashionable, and more permanent theatres were erected in the West End. Yet when, after a century of discussion, Britain's first National Theatre was built in 1976, it was appropriate that

ABOVE ELIZABETHAN THEATRES PROVIDED SHELTER FOR THE AUDIENCE BUT NOT THE PLAYERS. THIS DRAWING IS BELIEVED TO SHOW THE ROSE THEATRE IN SOUTHWARK, NEAR SHAKESPEARE'S GLOBE.

RIGHT FIREWORKS OUTSIDE THE DUKE OF RICHMOND'S HOUSE IN WHITEHALL, 1749.

RE-WORKES and ILLVMINATIONS, at his GRACE the Duke of RICHMOND'S at WHITE-HALL and on the River Thames, on Monday 15 May, 1749. Perform'd by the direction of Charles Frederick Esq.

Corded Mortars with Air Ballons
D.° with Sucifsons.
Flights of Sky Rocketts.
Pots de Brin.
Water Rocketts.
Jatte d'eau.
Water Ballons with 3 Stages of Lights.
Vertical Illumination

VE des FEUX d'ARTIFICE et des ILLUMINATIONS donneés par Monseigneur le Duc de RICHMOND de LENOX et d'AUBIGNY. sur la TAMISE et vis a vis de son Hotel. Lundi le 15.ieme de Mai 1749. Sous la direction de Mons. Frederick a Londre.

N°. Le Pavillon magnifiquement Illuminé,
2. L'Hotel de Mons.r Le Duc de Richmond.
3. Les Bateaux employés aux Feux d'artifices Aquatique.
A. Barque de sa Majesté.

serious drama should return to its riverside roots, little more than a mile upstream from Bankside.

No sooner had the theatres moved away from the south bank in the mid-seventeenth century than they were replaced by a new leisure trend, the public pleasure gardens. Until then the delight of strolling in a landscaped garden, adorned with classical sculptures and stately trees, was available only to those wealthy enough to have large houses and gardens of their own. Now, for a few pennies, Londoners of modest means could emulate them.

Cuper's Garden, on three acres of land now occupied by the southern approach to Waterloo Bridge, appears to have been London's first garden of this nature. It was opened in the 1630s by Abraham Cuper, a servant of the Earl of Arundel, who owned the land. In 1686 it was greatly extended, and it remained open until 1760, when it was shut down by the authorities because it had become a haunt of pickpockets. By then it had anyway been outshone by Vauxhall Gardens, a couple of miles upstream, which opened as the New Spring Gardens in 1660.

Vauxhall was the best-known and longest-lived of London's pleasure gardens, surviving until 1859. People took wherries from the City and Westminster across the river to stroll in its shaded avenues, dally in its arbours, look at works of art and listen to music, for which it was renowned. As Pepys noted, there was in the early years no charge for admission, but refreshments were expensive and portions notoriously small: there was a joke that a Vauxhall waiter could cover the whole of the gardens' eleven acres with paper-thin slices from a single ham.

THE GRAND WALK AT VAUXHALL GARDENS IN THE 18TH CENTURY.

Like many of London's public areas it soon gained a licentious reputation, and in 1712 Addison wrote that it would be improved if there were 'more nightingales and fewer strumpets'. Yet there were also fine paintings and sculptures to be seen, among them works by Hogarth and Roubiliac, and the gardens were still presenting concerts of high quality. In 1749 a rehearsal of Handel's music for the royal fireworks was given there before twelve thousand people.

Fireworks themselves became part of the entertainment in the late eighteenth century, and the fare on offer was broadened to include variety acts, such as acrobats and jugglers, and even balloon ascents.

For a while the word 'Vauxhall' passed into the language to mean a pleasure garden of this nature, for smaller ones borrowed the name when they opened in provincial towns. Only with the rapid expansion of London's population in the mid-nineteenth century, and the opening of Vauxhall Bridge, did the land occupied by the gardens become more valuable for housing and for railway construction than for entertainment. All that now remains of the former gardens is the manager's house in Kennington Lane, a Georgian building that later served

as the vicarage of St Peter's Church across the road.

Vauxhall had rivals north of the river. Ranelagh Gardens in Chelsea opened in 1742, in what were the grounds of Lord Ranelagh's house, and featured a large covered rotunda so that it could stage concerts in all weathers. The gardens themselves stretched down to the river bank, and one of the earliest regattas on the Thames was held there in 1775. Cremorne Gardens, where Lots Road power station now stands, flourished briefly in the nineteenth century, when, like Vauxhall, it became known for the glamour and availability of the single women who frequented it.

Down river, and back on the south bank, Rotherhithe was in the eighteenth and nineteenth centuries famous for 'tea gardens' – China Hall (still the name of a pub on the site), St Helena (whose musical evenings were patronized by the Prince Regent) and Island House, now Southwark Park, where visitors used to sail along mill streams in small boats. By the end of the nineteenth century all were gone, and Londoners in search of such pleasures had to take the river steamers to Rosherville, near Gravesend.

Traditionally, beverages stronger than tea are associated with life on the

CREMORNE GARDENS AT CHELSEA WAS FAMOUS FOR ITS HIGH-CLASS COURTESANS.

water. Seamen downed rum to combat the cold and other hardships, and that led to a tolerant attitude towards alcohol on all ships and boats. On the river banks, scores of public houses catered for those who used the river and worked in the docks and wharves and, later, for people who merely wanted to drink while enjoying its views. Some were licensed to open at breakfast time to meet the requirements of the dockers.

Wapping, Limehouse, Rotherhithe, Charlton and Greenwich all had their clusters of sailors' pubs, and a few remain. The Town of Ramsgate and the Prospect of Whitby in Wapping were named in honour of the home ports of boats that called there regularly. The Grapes, in Limehouse's Narrow Street, was the pub described as the Six Jolly Fellowship Porters by Dickens in *Our Mutual Friend*.

Many of the dockers' pubs on the Isle of Dogs have closed and been pulled down now that the docks have gone, but two notable examples remain: the Ferry Boat Inn, where the ferry from Greenwich used to make its landfall, and the Watermen's Arms on the east side of the Isle, which in the 1960s drew crowds from all over London to its evenings of Victorian music hall. The new office developments at Canary Wharf and South Quay include several modern pubs at the water's edge.

Across the river the Trafalgar and the Cutty Sark (formerly the Union) are among several popular pubs in Greenwich. Until 1857 the Trafalgar was the venue for the annual whitebait festival and fair which ran for three days every Easter and was one of the highlights of the east London year. It ended when the river became too polluted for whitebait to be caught in it.

The Mayflower in Rotherhithe stands where the Pilgrim Fathers set sail for Plymouth on their way to America. There has been a pub there since the sixteenth century. Formerly called the Spread Eagle and Crown, its name was changed to that of the pilgrims' boat in the 1950s. The Angel, near King's Stairs on the eastern edge of Bermondsey, is the successor to an even earlier hostelry, the Salutation, established in the fifteenth century.

Further upstream, the Anchor at Bankside, formerly associated with the adjacent Barclay's Brewery, which has now gone, remains a popular resort for Londoners on warm summer evenings. East of Blackfriars Bridge, the Founder's Arms also boasts good river views, and hard by the bridge, seeming almost as it if were built into it, is the modern Doggett's Coat and Badge, named after the annual watermen's boat race which begins at London Bridge and ends at Chelsea. At piers in the City and around Charing Cross, a few boats, permanently moored, have been turned into pubs or restaurants.

As you move up river, beyond the range of the large seagoing ships and their boisterous crews, the riverside pubs have always been more genteel. In Chelsea there are one or two within sight of the river along Cheyne Walk, but none that actually backs on to it. For that you have to wait for the Star and Garter at Putney and a string of pleasant Victorian inns on the north bank at Hammersmith. After that they occur regularly every mile at least.

These are all river*side* pleasures. The range of delights to be enjoyed on

THE TRAFALGAR TAVERN AT GREENWICH WAS THE VENUE FOR THE POPULAR WHITEBAIT FESTIVAL, HELD EVERY EASTER UNTIL THE RIVER BECAME TOO POLLUTED FOR THE FISH.

the water itself is necessarily more limited. Formal pageants are now rare. Marinas on the new developments in Docklands and Chelsea are growing increasingly popular with weekend sailors, although, despite the fall in commercial traffic, there are still enough monster vessels in the river's lower reaches to daunt many owners of little boats. Above Putney, messing about in boats grows more popular. On all stretches, vessels are increasingly hired for private or business functions.

The boat race between Oxford and Cambridge Universities is one of the few annual events focused on the river itself. It was inaugurated in 1829 at

HAMMERSMITH BRIDGE ON
BOAT RACE DAY, BY WALTER
GREAVES.

Henley but was not contested again for seven years, when it was switched to central London, between Westminster and Putney. Because of river traffic congestion it moved again in 1864, to the present course, four miles and 374 yards long, between Putney and Mortlake, and soon became established as an early spring occasion for popular celebration out of all proportion to the importance or interest of the event itself.

Hammersmith Bridge, roughly half way, provides a good, if fleeting view of the oarsmen heaving painfully to gain an extra yard. By the 1870s between eleven and twelve thousand people crammed on to it every boat race day – an important reason why the bridge had to be replaced in the 1880s. Everyone took sides, favouring one or other of the crews for quite arbitrary reasons. Drinking and carousing in the riverside pubs continued long after the race was over, and after dark many revellers went on to celebrate in the West End.

Today the Boat Race, now televised live, continues to arouse great interest but has become less of a pretext for licentiousness.

The rarest and most eagerly anticipated of river celebrations were the 'frost fairs' which occurred once or twice every century until 1831, when the removal of Old London Bridge allowed the river above it to flow too fast to freeze solid.

Even before that, it needed several days of exceptionally low temperatures to make the ice sufficiently hard to bear the weight of stalls, sideshows and the thousands of people who sought the unusual experience of walking from one side of the river to the other without the benefit of a bridge.

Watermen are said to have initiated the frost fairs to compensate for the revenue they were losing while unable to ferry people across. They manned many of the stalls and some even hitched horses to their boats, charging people to ride in these makeshift sleighs. The first frost fair recorded with certainty was in 1564-5, and the longest was in 1683-4, lasting three months, with a bullring among the attractions erected on the ice. The diarist John Evelyn described the proceedings that year as 'bacchanalian'. There were two fairs in the first half of the eighteenth century and the last took place in 1814.

As London's river became industrialized in the eighteenth century, it and its banks were used less and less for enjoyment. Instead, it became a means of escape, down to the seaside resorts at its mouth. It was not until after the Second World War that it began to regain its festive air. The catalyst was the Festival of Britain in 1951, the symbol of the nation's peacetime resurgence. This took place on the south bank near Waterloo Station. London's premier concert hall, the Royal Festival Hall, was built in conjunction with it and has become the focal point of an arts complex that now includes a second, smaller concert hall, the Hayward art gallery, the National Theatre, the National Film Theatre and the Museum of the Moving Image.

Up river at Battersea a funfair and pleasure gardens were created as another Festival attraction, lasting into the 1980s. Plans to build an indoor amusement park in the shell of the imposing Battersea Power Station have been suspended for financial reasons, but not entirely abandoned.

Along with the revival of these riparian attractions, provision has been made for the simplest of the river's pleasures – walking alongside it. Nearly all the new developments on either bank include a public footpath. As a result it is now possible, for example, to walk along a dedicated path, with only a few gaps, nearly all the way from Battersea to Deptford, taking in alluring views of river life and calling along the way at clusters of modern shops, cafés and stalls. There is no more apt symbol of the reclamation of the Thames for Londoners' enjoyment.

THE CLOSURE OF THE DOCKS HAS BROUGHT NEW LEISURE OPPORTUNITIES FOR LONDONERS. PART OF THE OLD MILLWALL DOCK IS NOW A CENTRE FOR WINDSURFING AND OTHER WATER SPORTS.

CHAPTER ELEVEN

IMAGES OF THE RIVER

Earth has not anything to show more fair; Dull would he be of soul who could pass by A sight so touching in its majesty: This City now doth, like a garment, wear The beauty of the morning; silent, bare, Ships, towers, domes, theatres, and temples lie Open unto the fields, and to the sky; All bright and glittering in the smokeless air.

WILLIAM WORDSWORTH, 1807

PREVIOUS PAGES WILLIAM DANIELL (1769-1837) PAINTED MANY VIEWS OF THE THAMES ESTUARY BUT ALSO OF THE RIVER ABOVE LONDON, SUCH AS THIS ONE AT RICHMOND.

THE RIVER has long exerted a hold on artists. One of the earliest surviving views of London dates from the fifteenth century and depicts Charles, Duke of Orleans, writing at a table in the Tower, where he was imprisoned for 25 years after the Battle of Agincourt. The picture, illustrating a book of the Duke's poems, has rowing boats of varying lengths plying the choppy waters in front of the Tower, while London Bridge is in the background, surmounted by a cluster of houses.

A century later Anthony van den Wyngaerde, from the Netherlands, drew a revealing panorama of the City and Westminster, seen from the south bank. Another Dutchman, Nicholas Visscher, provided a more detailed view in 1616, from Southwark. It shows the city dominated by the squat tower of old St Paul's Cathedral while, in the river, numerous boats are heading up-stream, driven by what appears to be an easterly wind. A three-masted galleon is the largest vessel portrayed, and just opposite St Paul's is a boat described in the contemporary caption as an 'eel ship', presumably from Visscher's native land.

Landscape painting did not become established in Britain until the seventeenth century, pioneered by Wenceslaus Hollar, a water-colourist and printmaker from Prague who had been brought to London in 1636 by Thomas Howard, Earl of Arundel. Hollar stayed at Arundel House, on the Strand, and often used it as a vantage-point. His most complete portrait of riverside London was drawn from the roof of St Saviour's Church in Southwark (now Southwark Cathedral): in the foreground, on the south bank, are Winchester Palace and the Bankside theatres. The picture brings out the width of the river compared to today, with dozens of small boats scurrying up, down and across it.

After the Restoration, when the romantic concept of rural landscapes took hold, artists started to recognize the picturesque quality of the river above the City. Another Dutchman, Jacob Knyff from Haarlem, painted scenes around Chiswick as, nearly fifty years later, did Pieter Rysbrack the Younger, best known for his view of Richmond Ferry. Frost fairs were so unusual that they inevitably attracted the attention of visiting painters: Robert Hondius gave a pictorial account of the long freeze of 1683-4, with horse-drawn coaches and sailing boats, manually tugged, using the ice as a highway.

One of the first considerable British-born landscape artists was Richard Wilson. Apart from his notable portrayals of Wales and Italy, he also worked in the Richmond area and at Marble Hill, near Twickenham, of which he painted four views around 1762. He liked to get right on to the banks to catch the full flavour of the river, where previous artists had preferred to look down on it from adjacent hills. His 1744 view of Westminster Bridge under construction is packed with detail and even has bathers enjoying themselves in the shallows. In his later works, Wilson sometimes took liberties with the topography, omitting buildings that detracted from his idealized romantic version. His contemporaries John Feary and George Samuel produced some notable views of Greenwich.

These artists were outshone in their time by Antonio Canaletto, who toured Britain between 1745 and 1755 and painted Thames views with the meticulous detail and balance that had characterized his work in Venice. He lived for much of his stay with the Duke of Richmond in Whitehall, and painted the river from that and nearby locations. Like so many others, he was captivated by Wren's naval hospital at Greenwich, which he celebrated in a painting of extraordinary vigour, recording the bustle of the boats and boatmen in a view from the southern tip of the Isle of Dogs.

The Englishman Samuel Scott was influenced by Canaletto. He began his career as a marine artist, but switched to urban and suburban riverscapes as a response to the Italian's success. Scott's view of the entrance to the Fleet River, just before it was paved over in 1760, has a distinctly Venetian feel to it, with the angular footbridge crossing the tributary, and wherries and spritsail barges milling around its mouth. Three of his Thames pictures hang in the Tate Gallery: one is a view downstream from Westminster Bridge, using the arch to frame the houses along Whitehall; another shows the waterside buildings at Nine Elms, including a timber yard, a kiln, and two windmills in the distance at Battersea; the third is a busy scene looking downstream at Cuckold's Point in Rotherhithe. William Marlow, a pupil of Scott, was likewise attracted to the river as a subject.

CHISWICK GARDENS BY PIETER RYSBRACK THE YOUNGER (1666-1729).

WILLIAM HOGARTH (1697-1764)
ENJOYED PORTRAYING
SCENES OF RIBALDRY AND
EXCESS, SUCH AS THIS
IMPRESSION OF SOUTHWARK
FAIR, SHUT DOWN BY THE
CITY FATHERS IN 1763.

William Hogarth, who lived and is buried by the river at Chiswick, preferred painting people to landscapes but qualifies as a Thames artist because his pictures were among the chief attractions of Vauxhall Gardens in the mid-eighteenth century. More than fifty years later Thomas Rowlandson, whose narrative paintings, drawings and caricatures were very much in the Hogarth tradition, produced a series of vivid pictures of the throng at Vauxhall, as well as Ranelagh opposite, and of livelier scenes up and down river at Eel Pie Island and Greenwich. His portraits of watermen made it easy to understand their uncouth reputation. His younger contemporary George Cruikshank recorded the last frost fair in 1814.

It is to the early nineteenth century marine artists that we owe our knowledge of the crush of sailing ships in the Pool of London that made the building of the docks essential. Fascinated with the fine detail of the vessels and their rigging, painters such as James Wilson Carmichael, Thomas Luny and Robert Havell gave a vivid impression of the impenetrable forest of masts below London Bridge, with the low rowing boats scurrying like ants around and between them. William Daniell produced some revealing views of the estuary for his series 'A Voyage Around Britain', painted in the first years of the nineteenth century.

John Constable, England's most popular landscape painter, is not best known for his London views, but he did undertake one monumental Thames work, celebrating the opening of Waterloo Bridge in 1817. Here the pageantry rather than the river itself is the central theme, with the Prince Regent ceremonially processing towards the state barge at Whitehall Stairs, and even the bridge assuming a low profile in the middle distance. Constable was never

truly satisfied with the painting – which is perhaps why it was not exhibited until 1832 – and he seldom returned to London's river as a source of inspiration.

Joseph Turner was born a year earlier than Constable, in 1775. His fascination with the effect of light on water is manifested in his sea and river paintings. His first work exhibited, when he was fifteen, was a watercolour of Lambeth Palace, and another of his early paintings depicted Millbank. He returned to the Thames again and again. In the first decade of the nineteenth century he made numerous studies of the river between Richmond and Twickenham and in 1819 produced a large canvas, some ten feet wide, showing the Thames winding beneath Richmond Hill, where a crowd had gathered to celebrate the Prince Regent's birthday.

Like Canaletto before him, Turner was impressed by the grandeur of Wren's Greenwich hospital and portrayed it several times, notably in an 1809 painting of London from the top of Greenwich Hill. This is in the Clore Gallery

THE ENTRANCE TO THE FLEET RIVER BY SAMUEL SCOTT (1702-1772).

at the Tate, along with several of the watercolours of the river he painted in the early 1820s as part of a projected series of London pictures. (One of these, showing Old London Bridge, is in the Victoria and Albert.) The Cleveland Museum of Art in Ohio has one of his most powerful river paintings, showing the burning of the Houses of Parliament in 1834, the orange flames roaring skyward and reflected in the calm water. Four years later, Nelson's warship *Téméraire*, as it was towed to the breaker's yard in Rotherhithe by a tall-funnelled paddle steamer, inspired one of Turner's best-loved paintings, now hanging in the National Gallery. John Ruskin wrote of *The Fighting Téméraire*: 'The utmost pensiveness which can ordinarily be given to a landscape depends on adjuncts of ruin: but no ruin was ever so affecting as this gliding of the vessel to her grave.'

Born in Covent Garden, Turner lived near the Thames for much of his life. In his youth he divided his time between London and Brentford. From 1806 to 1811 he had a cottage at Upper Mall in Chiswick, and later he lived from time to time at his father's old house in Twickenham. From 1839 until his death in 1851 he was one of a colony of artists who established themselves at or near Cheyne Walk, on the Chelsea waterfront. Several of his later works have that part of the river as their subject and he occasionally used the tower of St Mary's, Battersea, as a vantage-point.

At around the same time John Varley was working at Chelsea and elsewhere on the Thames, mainly with watercolours. He taught, too, at the Mechanics' Institute, where among his pupils was William Holman Hunt, later a founder of the Pre-Raphaelite movement. The Pre-Raphaelites also based themselves in Chelsea: Hunt, Dante Gabriel Rossetti, John Millais and Edward Burne-Jones all lived in the vicinity at one time or another, although in their work they preferred rural to river scenes. So did Helen Allingham, another Cheyne Walk resident, whose water-colours of the gardens of Chelsea Hospital established her reputation for idyllic country compositions.

Those among the Chelsea Set who did use the river as a subject at this time were Philip Wilson Steer and the American James McNeill Whistler, who lived there for thirty years from 1860. It provided Whistler with the setting for his flamboyant *Nocturnes* series of river paintings, some of which show the lights of the Cremorne pleasure garden in the last year or so of its existence.

Whistler was idolized by Walter Greaves, a true Chelsea painter whose father, a ferryman and boat repairer in Cheyne Walk, had often rowed Turner across the river. In his naïve style, Greaves painted some accomplished river scenes, full of vivacity, notably *Hammersmith Bridge on Boat Race Day* and *Chelsea Regatta*, which shows people crowding near the water's edge by Cheyne Walk, before it was embanked. Down river, the port still attracted artists keen to portray the workaday world, with the smoke of steamships adding an extra element to the atmosphere.

ABOVE JAMES WHISTLER'S (1834-1903) NOCTURNE IN BLUE AND GOLD, ONE OF A SERIES OF NIGHT-TIME RIVER STUDIES, SHOWS A PIER OF OLD BATTERSEA BRIDGE AT LOW TIDE.

LEFT THE FIGHTING TEMERAIRE BY JOSEPH TURNER (1775-1851).

Sometimes the increasingly industrialized river would be used as a symbol of desolation. In 1858 Augustus Egg exhibited a suite of three narrative paintings at the Royal Academy, portraying the fate of a formerly prosperous young woman suddenly made homeless. The third picture shows her taking refuge by night beneath the arch of a boathouse off the Strand, dimly lit by a gas lamp, with the factory and shot tower on the south bank stark and forbidding in the moonlight. Gustave Doré, whose drawings helped spread awareness of the squalor of London's Victorian tenements, produced many scenes of working life in the docks.

Doré was one of a number of French artists drawn to London in the nineteenth century. The Impressionist Claude Monet paid a productive visit in

CLAUDE MONET (1840-1926)
PAINTED MANY STUDIES OF
THE OLD WATERLOO
BRIDGE, WITH INDUSTRIAL
SOUTHWARK BEYOND, FROM
HIS ROOMS AT THE SAVOY
HOTEL DURING HIS STAY IN
LONDON IN 1871.

1871, when he fled from Paris to avoid the repercussions of the Franco-Prussian war. Staying at the Savoy Hotel, overlooking Waterloo Bridge, he produced a number of shimmering views of the Houses of Parliament and the river overlain with mist. One is in the National Gallery, hung close to a view of St Paul's from the south bank painted two years later by Monet's compatriot Charles-François Daubigny, who was in London for the same reason. From a vantage-point approximately where the National Theatre now stands, Daubigny portrays the cathedral behind Blackfriars Bridge, with a fleet of flat-bottomed barges in the foreground. Another French artist, Alfred Sisley, painted a regatta scene on the Thames, which hangs in the Louvre.

In the present century the river has continued to prove a powerful inspiration. Artists such as Mary Potter, Maureen Black and Robert Colquhoun were and are repeatedly drawn to it, as was the Austrian expressionist Oscar Kokoschka. For some fifty years, from the 1920s to the 1970s, he painted numerous pictures of London's river. The Tate Gallery exhibits a glowing example, painted in 1959, when the artist positioned himself on the roof of Shell-Mex House in the Strand, looking down river at Waterloo Bridge, with St Paul's Cathedral in the distance. Eight years later he drew nine Thames scenes for a series of lithographs.

Victor Pasmore, born in 1908, lived in Hammersmith and Chiswick and for many years worked by the river as well, as a clerk for the London County Council at County Hall. The Thames riverscapes he painted early in his career were reminiscent of Whistler and Turner, but he made his name later as an abstract painter. In the latter half of the century, Geoffrey Fletcher's pen-and-ink sketches of London, featured in the *Daily Telegraph* and elsewhere,

ONE OF A NUMBER OF
THAMES VIEWS BY OSCAR
KOKOSCHKA (1886-1980).

include numerous Thames scenes, some of which were collected in his book, *London's River*, published in 1966.

Advertising posters offered new scope for illustrative art. The railway and steamboat companies, and especially the newly created London Transport, promoted their services in the early twentieth century by commissioning spirited though sometimes idealized paintings of city and suburban views, many featuring the river and its bucolic attractions.

Today artists of varying talent and quality continue to try to capture the essence of the Thames. Painters and sketchers sell their work to tourists, to newspapers and magazines, to book publishers and to local residents. The developers of many of the new projects being built along the river appoint their own 'official' artists and photographers. Its constantly shifting moods make the river an elusive target for those who seek in their work to define the true nature of the beast; but their attempts have enriched our consciousness and our artistic inheritance.

A S THE 1990s began, the distinct outlines of the new east London riverscape were starting to emerge from the mists of confusion and controversy that were bound to arise after such a radical upheaval as the closure of the vast docks complex. The Thames was about to enter yet another phase of its relationship with the capital, playing a different but no less vital part in its life and commerce.

For nearly two thousand years, the river had physically carried trade to the heart of London and this in turn had attracted industries of all kinds along its banks. Now those functions had been rendered obsolete. Modern distribution methods called for new techniques in new locations. But the approach of the 21st Century also brought innovations in the way that other and newer forms of commerce were undertaken. The movement of money and the trading of securities were becoming more and more sophisticated. It was in some respects fitting that the future centre for these growing businesses should be created above the redundant debris of the old trading system.

Indeed the scale and pace of the change in Docklands today is comparable in scope with the massive developments of the nineteenth century, which saw the emergence of London's docks as the commercial entrepôt of the world. Like the docks, the new developments will provide employment for tens of thousands of people. In addition, though, they will create living and leisure space on a scale that could not have been envisaged as recently as two decades ago, when the docks were reaching the end of their useful life.

There is another, more fundamental difference between Docklands of today and yesterday. The old docks were deliberately built behind high walls and so sustained a community and a life of their own, separate from the rest of the city and in a sense alien to it. They effectively barred access to the river which had, until then, been an integral part of the life of the capital. By contrast the new Docklands, and Canary Wharf in particular, has restored Londoners' interrupted relationship with their river. The many public spaces are designed to blend with and take advantage of their waterside setting. Some workers, residents and visitors will use the river as their regular means of access. And far from being remote from the traditional heart of the city, the new roads, tunnels and railways will bring it as close as ten minutes away.

The new Docklands is dominated by the striking 50-storey Canary Wharf Tower, designed by the American architect Cesar Pelli, at the heart of the world's most ambitious commercial development. It was Pelli who designed Olympia and York's most successful scheme to date, the World Financial Centre near the southern tip of Manhattan. There, as in London, a striking addition to the cityscape has been created on a riverside site made redundant by changes in the shipping industry. The Canary Wharf Tower is not merely a symbol of the dynamics behind the project but also continues the tradition of the Thames as a setting for imposing architectural landmarks, both functional and spectacular: the Tower, the Abbey, the Houses of Parliament, the bridges and even the sturdy warehouses.

When completed at a cost of some £4bn, the 26 buildings on the 71-acre site will provide ten million square feet of office space, half a million square feet of shops, restaurants, pubs and leisure facilities, with jobs for some fifty thousand people. It is different in scale from any other single development yet attempted in London. Its sheer size will affect the city's identity in much the same way as the development of the great estates of Belgravia, Bloomsbury and Mayfair established the character of the West End in earlier centuries. It will accommodate a new, self-sufficient community of its own, with a public meeting hall and several squares to provide focal points for public life. Docklands will in effect be a new town, and Canary Wharf is the critical mass on which the other parts of the development depend. Along with the West End and the City, it will provide a third hub for London's commercial and social life.

In addition to Pelli, many other international architects have worked on the scheme. The styles are varied with exterior detailing that harks back to nineteenth century city centres and to the best of the old warehouses – a few of

CABOT SQUARE IS THE FOCAL POINT OF THE NEW CANARY WHARF.

which have been preserved in Limehouse, Wapping and Rotherhithe. The new buildings have street-level arcades which will house some of its 250 shops, and the central plazas will contain fountains, trees and shrubs. The idea is to create a human-scale environment for day-to-day business, rather than to awe visitors and workers with excessive emphasis on size and grandeur.

The five stages of the project are being tackles roughly from west to east. The first phase, ready for occupation in the summer of 1991, includes Westferry Circus, with its pier for the river bus, and Cabot Square, graced by the 50-storey Tower. The pier will establish a new point of river activity, like those at Greenwich, Charing Cross, Westminster and Waterloo. Passengers will go up from it to a broad pedestrian esplanade running the quarter-mile length of the Canary Wharf riverfront. From there they will ascend again to Westferry Circus, which forms an upper terrace overlooking the river. Pedestrians will reign supreme, for traffic will be kept away from the public space at the river's edge.

Just north is Port East, a leisure and shopping area with a covered market, a multi-screen cinema and a hotel, built around a large block of early nineteenth-century warehouses and connected to the main development by a bridge over the water. The next two phases, Canada Square and Churchill Place, will take the scheme to its most easterly point, where Cartier Circle and an approach road join it to the new Limehouse Link. The final phase is back at the western end, north and south of Westferry Circus along the riverfront, where the buildings flanking the formal entry to the complex from the Thames will be substantially residential. The esplanade will be edged by low-rise blocks echoing in their height and form the six-storey warehouses characteristic of the Thames below the Tower. When completed by 1997, they will create two residential neighbourhoods focused on quiet squares in the manner that has been a feature of London planning since the late seventeenth century.

AN ATRIUM ADDS LIGHT AND INTIMACY TO THE MODERN OFFICE BUILDINGS.

Not only has Canary Wharf revived the northern part of the Isle of Dogs, it has also – at least temporarily – restored the river as a means of industrial transport. Some eighty per cent of the materials for the skyscraper and the other buildings have come up river from a holding warehouse at Tilbury, avoiding the need for fleets of heavy lorries which would have disrupted traffic for miles around. The level of shipping does not approach that in the old docks thirty years earlier, but on busy days, with timber and marble being winched up from the barges, it is possible to sense something of the old working atmosphere.

What will it be like to work in Canary Wharf once the offices begin to be occupied? The existing Docklands developments, around South Quay and Crossharbour stations, given an idea of what to expect, although until Canary

Wharf is functioning they are in effect a town without a centre. All the same, there is a sense of energy about the place. Talking to the people who work there is not like talking, say, to commodity dealers operating within the formal traditions of the City of London, or overseas bankers in the well-padded opulence of Mayfair, or the raffish folk in film, theatre and advertising who inhabit Soho and the West End. There are elements of all three in Docklands but the prevailing spirit is one of experiment and innovation. The move to this distinctive environment has encouraged fresh approaches.

Vicki Furey is an archetypal Docklands businesswoman. A journalist from New Zealand, she began working on the Isle of Dogs in 1981, before any of the new development began, and does not now like to contemplate going to work anywhere else. First a reporter on a Docklands newspaper, then press officer for the LDDC, she is now with MSP Communications, a public relations company, organising sponsored events from its base at South Quay.

As she looked north from her firm's conference room across West India Dock, to the Canary Wharf tower a few hundred yards away, she said: 'I'm one of the group that's been around for ever and a day and have seen the progress. In 1981-2 we thought they were absolute lunatics to talk even about workshops and three-storey buildings. . . . There weren't any roads – you just drove along the quayside. It only became civilised when they built the red brick road in 1984.

'The new people who are moving into the offices now come from the West End and the City where there are shops and fripperies and things and a few complain that it isn't like that here yet: whereas people like us couldn't believe it when Asda opened – a supermarket was a major event. It's a very insular community. When you've been through it you're very committed to it.'

THE DOCKLANDS LIGHT RAILWAY, OPENED BY THE QUEEN IN 1987, PROVIDES FAST TRANSPORT FOR DOCKLANDS COMMUTERS, AS WELL AS SPECTACULAR RIVERSIDE VIEWS.

Ian Spero is another enthusiast. He is a communications consultant working, like Ms Furey, in a comparatively new branch of the public relations industry, advising on sponsorship and promotion. After working in the United States he was looking for a place to live and was drawn to the Isle of Dogs.

'One freezing weekend my wife and I came down to have a look,' he recalls. 'The development we wanted wasn't ready and we were pointed to a caravan behind the Asda superstore. We waded through three or four inches of mud. We were shown some plans for new property to be built. We decided to put down our £100 and buy our house and in the summer of 1984 we moved in.'

Before long he decided it would be a suitable place for his office as well. That summer saw the construction of Skylines, one of the Isle's first purpose-built office developments, whose low pyramid-shaped roofs are today hemmed in by newer, taller blocks.

'There was nothing here then except for those triangular buildings and the red brick road. You could see from one side of the island to the other. Parking was never a problem. It tickled my fancy. I thought: "We're establishing a new company and looking to create a new client base anyway." I thought the location reflected the style and pioneer nature of our business. I felt the *nouvelle ambiance* of Docklands would enable me to carve out a niche in a particular market in an area which was suitably different. . . .

'There are a lot of misconceptions about Docklands, especially about its transport. In the early days people would turn up for appointments either half an hour early or twenty minutes late. But the environment has helped the business. The river and water are invaluable assets.'

By 1988, when Spero moved his company to a larger and newer suite of offices in Meridian Gate nearby, a distinct business community was beginning to evolve. Back up services such as banks, office equipment suppliers and, most important, serious restaurants had now opened. Some old pubs – like the George, by the Crossharbour DLR station – had successfully adapted to the new clientele and some imaginatively designed new ones had opened, such as the Spinnaker at South Quay. The novelty of working in Docklands, combined with the rates and tax concessions being passed on by the developers in lower rentals or purchase prices, was attracting imaginative entrepreneurs like Spero.

Another of them was Paul Glander who, with his wife, had built a firm called Car Carrying, arranging car deliveries for manufacturers and companies with large leased fleets. By 1988 the business was growing by some forty per cent a year, with sixty full-time drivers. It was time to move from Wanstead.

'Clients love coming out here and riding on the railway,' he says. 'But of course all the businesses are very dependent on the success of Canary Wharf to keep up the value of our investment in the property.'

Not all the new business people on the Isle of Dogs came out to purpose-built office space. At the beginning of 1987, Bob Gordon brought his Trade Printing Company from Smithfield to an old tobacco warehouse in Cuba Street, just inland from West India Dock pier and a few hundred yards south of Canary Wharf. Many of the initial inconveniences have been cured, and as new businesses arrive on the Isle, all needing stationery, promotional material and the like, his potential customer base increases. Like Glander, Gordon believes that the long-term viability of the Isle of Dogs as a business venue depends on the success of Canary Wharf in bringing fresh enterprises to the immediate vicinity.

While the Isle of Dogs was virgin territory for these kinds of service businesses, it was in no sense a desert island. Some twelve thousand people lived there at the start of the 1980s, nearly all in rented council homes at the southern end. These long-standing island residents did not automatically regard the developments as unqualified progress. Docklands people are traditionally suspicious of outsiders, especially when they come wielding

THE CANARY WHARF DEVELOPMENT PROVIDES THIS TOWERING VIEW ACROSS THE WATER FROM SOUTH QUAY, THE FIRST OF THE NEW COMMERCIAL COMMUNITIES ON THE ISLE OF DOGS.

bulldozers and bearing promises of unimaginable prosperity for all.

Since the 1950s one of the most vociferous spokesmen for the islanders, ensuring that their voice has been heard during the long process of planning and development, has been Ted Johns, who at the end of 1990 was elected to serve a fresh term as chairman of the Association of Island Communities (AIC), of which he was a founder member in 1976. Johns stresses that he and his fellow campaigners are not Luddites: they are not opposed to all development on principle.

'When Canary Wharf was first proposed I said to my colleagues on the AIC that it was something we wanted in Docklands. We needed something with cohesion: before that, developments were piecemeal and ad hoc, with no overall plan. Then along came the Canary Wharf people with plans for a comprehensive development that would hang together. We saw it as something that would bring in the transport infrastructure that ought to have been in place beforehand. We welcomed it, although the scale was a bit overwhelming.'

The first developer to devise plans for Canary Wharf was the American G. Ware Travelstead, who had backing from two securities companies, Morgan Stanley and Credit Suisse First Boston. The initial enthusiasm shown by Johns and the islanders waned when they saw how few jobs would be provided for local people in the original plan, and the AIC began campaigning against it. Their finest hour came in 1986 when they disrupted the ground-breaking ceremony – in the presence of the Governor of the Bank of England and other dignitaries – by releasing sheep and bees among the guests and adorning the site with large banners.

A few months later the Travelstead consortium collapsed when the two securities companies decided not to share development costs – although they still plan to occupy office buildings at Canary Wharf – and in 1987 the site was taken over by Olympia and York, a Canadian company run by the brothers Paul, Albert and Ralph Reichmann, which had developed several large office and retailing projects in Canada, as well as the World Financial Center and other projects in New York. At Canary Wharf, Olympia and York proved more attentive to local concerns than their predecessors. They gave money to train island youngsters in construction work, then employed them when they had completed their training. They also contributed to Docklands education programmes. As their Community Affairs Officer they appointed Peter Wade, an island resident active in the AIC.

'There was a lot of animosity towards Peter when he took the job,' says Johns. 'Graffiti outside his house and that kind of thing. But he spoke to me before he decided to accept the Olympia and York offer. I advised him to take it, or it would go to an outsider. This way at least we have a toe in the door.' After Wade's appointment, the atmosphere between residents and developers improved. Initial hostility between the islanders and their neighbours in the new flats and houses was abating, too as there had been resentment that none of the new housing was for rental in the public sector.

'There was antagonism in the early days,' said Johns. 'There was abusive graffiti and some of the new people had their cars broken into. But it's better now. Those people who bought for the short term have come and gone but a lot of the others are committed to the place and have become members of the AIC. They need the same as we do – health centres, libraries and good transport.

'I think the time has come when we've got to stop scoring political points and got to start pulling Docklands up. It's a place capable of magnificent adventure. We've got to work with the LDDC and the developers and they've got to work with us, because Docklands is at stake and from the local people's point of view I don't think we'd ever forgive anyone who sold Docklands short.'

The same pride of place was in evidence across the river. In Bermondsey and Rotherhithe, the balance of redevelopment was towards housing rather

THESE GARDENS ARE AN INTEGRAL PART OF THE NEW DEVELOPMENT.

than commercial space. For two hundred years the river had been lined with warehouses and factories, while the people who worked in them lived in cramped and often insanitary terraces behind them, plagued with pollution and noise. Now, with the industry gone, they could claim the riverside for their own. After some political battles, about the balance between private and public housing, here too the community began to come together for the good of the area as a whole.

Apart from the new flats and houses, there were several innovations in what are broadly called leisure developments. The Design Museum at Shad

GREAT CARE HAS BEEN TAKEN WITH THE DETAIL OF THE STREET FURNITURE ON CANARY WHARF. THESE RAILINGS ARE AROUND THE GARDEN OF WESTFERRY CIRCUS, NEAR THE PIER FOR THE WATER BUS.

RIGHT THE ISLE OF DOGS, 1991, WITH GREENWICH IN THE FOREGROUND.

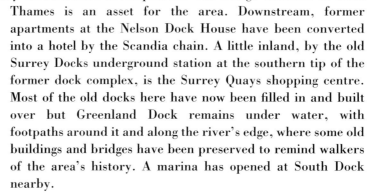

Thames is an asset for the area. Downstream, former apartments at the Nelson Dock House have been converted into a hotel by the Scandia chain. A little inland, by the old Surrey Docks underground station at the southern tip of the former dock complex, is the Surrey Quays shopping centre. Most of the old docks here have now been filled in and built over but Greenland Dock remains under water, with footpaths around it and along the river's edge, where some old buildings and bridges have been preserved to remind walkers of the area's history. A marina has opened at South Dock nearby.

Olympia and York plan an office complex in Surrey Docks when Canary Wharf is completed, by which time the extension of the Jubilee Line will pass through here. That will leave the Royal Docks, farther east on the north shore, as the last part of Docklands to be developed. Plans for a mixed scheme here, including the London Dome entertainment and conference centre, were delayed when the original developers pulled out in the depths of the 1989-90 recession, but the LDDC believe they will be revived. The eastwards extension of the Docklands Light Railway will reach there by 1992, while the Limehouse Link and the East India Dock Link, with a new crossing of the mouth of the River Lea, will greatly improve road access. The projected East London River Crossing would make it still easier to reach.

Says David Hardy, the LDDC chairman: 'I think the Royals will take a year to plan, a year to find the finance and more than a year to build. By that time the recession should be over. It's going to succeed. It's close to the City and the Channel Tunnel and the infrastructure will be here.'

When the last occupants move in to the Royals, the task the LDDC was set up to achieve will have been completed. To effect within twenty years so radical a transformation of the redundant docks, from acres of derelict land to a vibrant business and residential community, with Canary Wharf at its heart, will then be seen as an achievement as awe-inspiring in its way as any on the Thames since William the Conqueror began the White Tower. As the new century begins, London's river, responsive as ever to the tide of history, will be playing a renewed role in the service of the city it spawned.

BIBLIOGRAPHY

Anderson, Jo, *Anchor and Hope* Hodder & Stoughton, 1980.

Anderson, Romola and R. C., *The Sailing Ship* Evelyn, 1965 (new ed).

Barker, Felix and Jackson, Peter, *London, 2000 Years of a City and Its People* Cassell, 1974.

Broodbank, J. G., *History of the Port of London* (two vols.) Daniel O'Connor, 1921.

Brown, R. Douglas, *The Port of London* Terence Dalton, 1978.

Cameron, Robt, & Cooke, Alistair, *Above London* Bodley Head, 1980.

Chaplin, Peter H., *The Thames From Source To Tideway* Whippet Books, 1982.

Cherry, Bridget and Pevsner, Nikolaus, *The Buildings of England: London – South* Penguin, 1983.

Clark, John, *Saxon and Norman London*, HMSO, 1989.

Clegg, W. Paul, *Docks and Ports 2: London* Ian Allan, 1987.

Clunn, Harold P., *The Face of London* Spring Books, 1950

Cowie, Robert and Whytehead, Robert, *Lundenwic: The Archaeological Evidence For Middle Saxon London* Antiquity vol 63, no 241, 1989.

Cracknell, Basil E., *Portrait of London's River* Robert Hale, 1968.

Croad, Stephen, *London's Bridges* Royal Comm on Hist Monmnts, 1983.

Dix, Frank L., *Royal River Highway* David and Charles, 1985.

Dodd, George, *Days at the Factories* Charles Knight and Co., 1843.

Ellmers, Chris *City and River* Museum of London, 1989.

Ellmers, Chris, and Werner, Alex, *London's Lost Riverscape* Viking, 1988.

Fletcher, Geoffrey, *London's River* Hutchinson, 1966.

Gardiner, Dorothy, *The Story of Lambeth Palace* Constable, 1930.

Hemming, Charles, *British Landscape Painters* Gollancz, 1989.

Herbert, A. P., *The Thames* Weidenfeld and Nicholson, 1966.

Hostettler, Eve, *An Outline History of the Isle of Dogs* Island History Trust, 1988.

Howard, Philip, *London's River* Hamish Hamilton, 1975.

Kerrigan, Colin, *A History of Tower Hamlets* London Borough of Tower Hamlets Community Services, 1982.

Leapman, Michael (ed), *The Book of London* Weidenfeld & Nicholson, 1989.

London Borough of Southwark Neighbourhood Histories. *No. 6, The Story of Rotherhithe; No. 7, The Story of The Borough; No. 8, The Story of Bankside.*

Merrifield, Ralph, *The Roman City of London* Ernest Benn, 1965.

Milne, Gustav, *The Port of Roman London* Batsford, 1985.

Morris, John, *Londinium – London in the Roman Empire* Weidenfeld & Nicholson, 1982.

Nicholson, Louise, *London – Louise Nicholson's Definitive Guide* Bodley Head, 1988.

Pevsner, Nikolaus, *The Buildings of England: London 1 The Cities of London and Westminster* Penguin, 1957. Third edition, 1973.

Phillips, Geoffrey, *Thames Crossings* David and Charles, 1981.

Phillips, Tony, *A London Docklands Guide* Peter Marcan Publications, 1986.

Pudney, John, *Crossing London's River* Dent, 1972.

Pudney, John, *London's Docks* Thames and Hudson, 1975.

Schweitzer, Pam, and Wegner, Charles (eds), *On The River: Memories of a Working River* Age Exchange, 1989.

Stow, John, *The Survey of London* (first pub. 1603) Dent, 1987.

Unwin, George, *The Gilds and Companies of London* Methuen, 1908.

Weightman, Gavin, *London River* Collins and Brown, 1990.

Wilson, David G., *The Thames: Record of a Working Waterway* Batsford, 1987.

Wilson, Derek, *The Tower, 1078-1978* Hamish Hamilton, 1978.

Yule, Brian, *Excavations at Winchester Palace, Southwark* London Archaeologist, vol. 6, no. 2. Spring 1989.

ACKNOWLEDGEMENTS

Bridgeman Art Library: Albright Knox Art Gallery, New York 145; British Library 58; Chris Beetles Gallery 39; Christie's 41, 76-77, 133; Coram Foundation 46; David Messum Fine Paintings 136-137; Eaton Gallery 87; Fine Arts Society 56; Giraudon 23; Guildhall Library and Art Gallery 2, 31, 33, 36-37, 40, 42, 45, 50-51, 61, 62-63, 66-67, 70, 72, 89, 90-91, 93, 95, 97, 98-99, 101, 112-113, 115, 117, 118, 121, 127, 130, 141; Houses of Parliament 28-29; Hugh Lane Municipal Gallery of Modern Art, Dublin 144; Lloyds of London 65; Musée des Beaux Arts, Dieppe 84; Musée Taucet Delacour, Pontoise Laurois 59; Museum of London 131; Private Collection 32, 35, 128, 129; Royal Thames Yacht Club 81; Roy Miles Fine Paintings 48, 79, 139; Spink & Son 24-25; Tate Gallery 143; V & A 55.

British Library: 29.

British Museum: 16.

Hulton Picture Company: 53, 57, 69, 71, 73, 83, 96, 119, 120.

Mary Evans Picture Library: 22, 23, 30, 54, 95, 100.

Museum of London: 14-15, 17, 18, 20, 21, 82, 116.

National Gallery: 134.

Olympia & York: 107, 111, 146-147, 148-149, 150, 152-153, 155, 156, 157.

Susan Griggs Agency: Miles Clark 124-125; John Heseltine 1; John Marmaras 8-9; Storm Stanley 75; Adam Woolfitt 10, 11, 12, 13, 44, 49, 64, 74, 102-103, 105, 108, 109, 122, 123, 135, 151.

Tate Gallery: 134.

VISUAL RESEARCH: LYNDA MARSHALL

INDEX